GLENCOE MATHEMATICS

Teacher's An

MW01488403

TAKS Practice
and Sample Test
Workbook

Glencoe

New York, New York   Columbus, Ohio   Chicago, Illinois   Peoria, Illinois   Woodland Hills, California

Test-Taking Tips

- Go to bed early the night before the test. You will think more clearly after a good night's rest.

- Read each problem carefully and think about ways to solve the problem before you try to answer the question.

- Relax. Most people get nervous when taking a test. It's natural. Just do your best.

- Answer questions you are sure about first. If you do not know the answer to a question, skip it and go back to that question later.

- Think positively. Some problems may seem hard to you, but you may be able to figure out what to do if you read each question carefully.

- If no figure is provided, draw one. If one is furnished, mark it up to help you solve the problem.

- When you have finished each problem, reread it to make sure your answer is reasonable.

- Become familiar with a variety of formulas and when they should be used.

- Make sure that the number of the question on the answer sheet matches the number of the question on which you are working in your test booklet.

Glencoe

The **McGraw·Hill** Companies

Send all inquiries to:
The McGraw-Hill Companies
8787 Orion Place
Columbus, OH 43240-4027

ISBN: 0-07-845601-0

Grade 9 TAKS Practice
and Sample Test Workbook TAE

1 2 3 4 5 6 7 8 9 10   079   10 09 08 07 06 05 04 03

Contents

Mathematics Chart

	Metric	Customary
Length	1 kilometer = 1000 meters 1 meter = 100 centimeters 1 centimeter = 10 millimeters	1 mile = 1760 yards or 5280 feet 1 yard = 3 feet 1 foot = 12 inches

	Metric	Customary
Capacity and Volume	1 liter = 1000 milliliters	1 gallon = 4 quarts or 128 ounces 1 quart = 2 pints 1 pint = 2 cups 1 cup = 8 ounces

	Metric	Customary
Mass and Weight	1 kilogram = 1000 grams 1 gram = 1000 milligrams	1 ton = 2000 pounds 1 pound = 16 ounces

Time	1 year = 365 days = 12 months = 52 weeks	1 week = 7 days 1 day = 24 hours 1 hour = 60 minutes 1 minute = 60 seconds

Perimeter	rectangle	$P = 2\ell + 2w$	or $P = 2(\ell + w)$
Circumference	circle	$C = 2\pi r$	or $C = \pi d$
Area	rectangle	$A = \ell w$	or $A = bh$
	triangle	$A = \frac{1}{2}bh$	or $A = \frac{bh}{2}$
	trapezoid	$A = \frac{1}{2}(b_1 + b_2)h$	or $A = \frac{(b_1 + b_2)h}{2}$
	circle	$A = \pi r^2$	
Surface Area	cube	$S = 6s^2$	
	cylinder (lateral)	$S = 2\pi rh$	
	cylinder (total)	$S = 2\pi rh + 2\pi r^2$	or $S = 2\pi r(h + r)$
	cone (lateral)	$S = \pi r\ell$	
	cone (total)	$S = \pi r\ell + \pi r^2$	or $S = \pi r(\ell + r)$
	sphere	$S = 4\pi r^2$	
Volume	prism or cylinder	$V = Bh$	
	pyramid or cone	$V = \frac{1}{3}Bh$	
	sphere	$V = \frac{4}{3}\pi r^3$	

Pi	π	$\pi \approx 3.14$	or $\pi \approx \frac{22}{77}$

Pythagorean Theorem	$a^2 + b^2 = c^2$
Distance Formula	$d = \sqrt{(x_2 - x_1)^2 (y_2 - y_1)^2}$
Slope of a Line	$m = \frac{y_2 - y_1}{x_2 - x_1}$
Midpoint Formula	$M = \left(\frac{x_2 + x_1}{2}, \frac{y_1 - y_2}{2} \right)$
Quadratic Formula	$x = \frac{-b \pm \sqrt{b^2 - 4ac}}{2}$
Slope-Intercept Form of an Equation	$y = mx + b$
Point-Slope Form of an Equation	$y - y_1 = m(x - x_1)$
Standard Form of an Equation	$Ax + By = C$
Simple Interest Formula	$I = prt$

Correlation of Grade 9 TAKS Objectives to Glencoe's *Mathematics: Applications and Connections*, Course 3, *Pre-Algebra*, and *Algebra 1*

Texas Assessment of Knowledge and Skills (TAKS)	Algebra 1
Objective 1 The student will describe functional relationships in a variety of ways.	
A(b)(1)(A)	1-9, 3-2, 4-8, 5-3, 5-4, 5-5, 6-2, 6-3, 6-5, 11-1, 11-2, Inv. (pp. 68–69, 83, 111, 154, 177, 184), Inv. (pp. 190–191, 200, 227, 269, 302, 314), Inv. (pp. 448–449, 461, 519, 541, 548)
A(b)(1)(B)	1-9, 3-2, 3-3, 4-8, 5-2, 5-3, 5-4, 5-5, 5-6, 6-3, 6-4, 7-6, 11-4, 12-1, Inv. (pp. 68–69, 83, 111, 154, 177, 184), Inv. (pp. 190–191, 200, 227, 269, 302, 314), Inv. (pp. 320–321, 338, 361, 398, 426, 442), Inv. (pp. 448–449, 461, 519, 541, 548)
A(b)(1)(C)	5-4, 5-6, 6-4, 11-1, 11-2, 11-3, 11-4, 11-5, Inv. (pp. 190–191, 200, 227, 269, 302, 314), Inv. (pp. 320–321, 338, 361, 398, 426, 442), Inv. (pp. 448–449, 461, 519, 541, 548)
A(b)(1)(D)	1-9, 3-1A, 3-1, 3-2, 3-3A, 3-3, 3-4, 3-5, 3-6, 4-8, 5-2, 5-3, 5-4, 5-5, 5-6, 5-7, 6-2, 6-3, 6-4, 6-5, 7-1, 7-2A, 7-2, 7-3, 7-4, 7-6, 11-1, 11-2, 11-3, 11-4, 11-5, 12-1, Inv. (pp. 68–69, 83, 111, 154, 177, 184), Inv. (pp. 190–191, 200, 227, 269, 302, 314), Inv. (pp. 320–321, 338, 361, 398, 426, 442), Inv. (pp. 448–449, 461, 519, 541, 548), Inv. (pp. 656–657, 695, 718, 741, 748)
A(b)(1)(E)	1-9, 3-2, 3-3, 5-2, 5-3, 5-4, 5-5, 5-6, 6-3, 6-4, 6-5, 11-1, 11-2, 11-3, 11-4, 11-5, 12-1, Inv. (pp. 68–69, 83, 111, 154, 177, 184), Inv. (pp. 320–321, 338, 361, 398, 426, 442), Inv. (pp. 448–449, 461, 519, 541, 548), Inv. (pp. 554–555, 586, 600, 617, 627, 650)
Objective 2 The student will demonstrate an understanding of the properties and attributes of functions.	
A(b)(2)(A)	5-4, 6-5A, 6-6, 11-1B, 11-1
A(b)(2)(B)	1-9, 4-8, 5-2, 5-3, 5-4, 5-5, 11-1, Inv. (pp. 68–69, 83, 111, 154, 177, 184), Inv. (pp. 320–321, 338, 361, 398, 426, 442), Inv. (pp. 448–449, 461, 519, 541, 548), Inv. (pp. 554–555, 586, 600, 617, 627, 650)
A(b)(2)(C)	1-9, 2-1, 2-2, 5-1, 5-2, 5-3, 5-4, 5-5, 5-6, 6-1, 6-2, 6-3, 6-4, 6-5, 6-6, 6-7, 7-1, 7-4, 7-6, 7-7, 7-8, 8-1, 8-2, 8-3, 8-5, 11-1, 11-2, 11-5, 13-5, 13-6
A(b)(2)(D)	2-2, 4-4, 4-6, 6-3, 6-4, Inv. (pp. 68–69, 83, 111, 154, 177, 184), Inv. (pp. 190–191, 200, 227, 269, 302, 314), Inv. (pp. 320–321, 338, 361, 398, 426, 442), Inv. (pp. 448–449, 461, 519, 541, 548), Inv. (pp. 656–657, 695, 718, 741, 748)

Texas Assessment of Knowledge and Skills (TAKS)	Algebra 1
A(b)(3)(A)	1-1, 1-2, 1-3, 1-5, 1-6, 1-7, 1-8, 2-3, 2-4, 2-5, 2-6, 2-7, 2-8, 2-9, 3-1, 3-2, 3-3, 3-4, 3-5, 3-6, 4-1, 4-2, 4-3, 4-4, 4-5, 4-7, 4-8, 5-2, 5-3, 5-4, 5-5, 5-6, 6-1, 6-2, 6-3, 6-4, 6-5, 6-6, 6-7, 7-1, 7-2, 7-3, 7-4, 7-6, 7-7, 7-8, 8-1, 8-2, 8-3, 8-4, 8-5, 9-1, 9-2, 9-3, 9-4, 9-5, 9-6, 9-7, 9-8, 10-1, 10-2, 10-3, 10-4, 10-5, 10-6, 11-1, 11-2, 11-3, 11-4, 11-5, 12-1, 12-2, 12-3, 12-4, 12-5, 12-6, 12-7, 12-8, 13-1, 13-2, 13-3, 13-4, 13-5, 13-6
A(b)(3)(B)	1-2, 1-3, 2-5, 2-6, 2-7, 3-2, 4-8, 5-6, 9-1, 9-2, 11-4
A(b)(4)(A)	3-1, 3-2, 3-3, 3-5, 3-6, 5-5, 9-4, 9-5, 9-6, 9-7, 9-8, 10-1, 10-2, 10-3, 10-4, 10-5, Inv. (pp. 448–449, 461, 519, 541, 548), Inv. (pp. 554–555, 586, 600, 617, 627, 650)
A(b)(4)(B)	1-7, 1-8, 2-3, 2-5, 2-6, 2-7, 3-5, 3-6, 4-1, 5-5, 6-2, 6-3, 6-4, 6-6, 9-3, 9-5, 9-6, 9-7, 9-8, 10-2, 10-3
Objective 3 The student will demonstrate an understanding of linear functions.	
A(c)(1)(A)	5-4, 5-5, 5-6, 6-3, 11-4, Inv. (pp. 190–191, 200, 227, 269, 302, 314)
A(c)(1)(C)	5-1, 5-2, 5-3, 5-4, 5-5, 5-6, 5-7, 6-3, 6-6
A(c)(2)(A)	6-1, 6-2, 6-4
A(c)(2)(B)	6-1, 6-2, 6-3, 6-4, 6-5
A(c)(2)(C)	6-2, 6-4, 6-5A, 6-5
A(c)(2)(D)	6-2, 6-3, 6-4
A(c)(2)(E)	6-4, 6-5
A(c)(2)(F)	6-4, 6-5
A(c)(2)(G)	4-1A, 4-1, 4-2, 4-3, 4-4, 4-5, 4-6, 4-7, 4-8, 6-4, 6-5A, 6-5, Inv. (pp. 190–191, 200, 227, 269, 302, 314)
Objective 4 The student will formulate and use linear equations and inequalities.	
A(c)(3)(A)	3-1, 3-2, 3-3, 3-4, 3-5, 3-6, 4-1, 5-3, 5-4, 5-5, 5-6, 6-2, 6-3, 6-4, 7-1, 7-2, 7-3, 7-4, 7-6, 7-8, Inv. (pp. 68–69, 83, 111, 154, 177, 184)
A(c)(3)(B)	3-1A, 3-1, 3-2, 3-3A, 3-3, 3-4, 3-5, 3-6, 5-3, 5-5, 5-6, 6-3, 6-4, 7-1, 7-2A, 7-2, 7-3, 7-4, 7-6, 7-8, Inv. (pp. 320–321, 338, 361, 398, 426, 442)
A(c)(3)(C)	5-4, 6-4, 6-5, 7-1, 7-2, 7-3, 7-4, 7-6, 7-8
A(c)(4)(A)	8-1, 8-2, 8-3, 8-4, Inv. (pp. 448–449, 461, 519, 541, 548)
Objective 5 The student will demonstrate an understanding of quadratic and other nonlinear functions.	
A(d)(1)(C)	11-1B
A(d)(3)(A)	1-1, 1-2, 9-1, 9-2, 9-3, 11-4

Texas Assessment of Knowledge and Skills (TAKS)	Mathematics: Applications and Connections, Course 3	Pre-Algebra
Objective 6 The student will demonstrate an understanding of geometric relationships and spatial reasoning.		
(8.6)(A)	5-6A, 8-10	11-6
(8.6)(B)	8-10, 10-7, 10-8	11-9
(8.7)(D)	2-10, 4-6, 10-2, 10-4A, 10-4, 10-5, 10-6, 10-7, 10-8, 10-9	1-7, 2-2, 2-2B, 3-5B, 8-1, 8-2, 8-3, 8-3B, 8-4, 8-5, 8-6, 8-6B, 8-7, 8-8, 8-9, 11-9
Objective 7 The student will demonstrate an understanding of two-and three-dimensional representations of geometric relationships and shapes.		
(8.7)(A)	11-2A, 11-2	12-4, 12-7
(8.7)(B)	3-4B, 5-1, 5-2, 5-4, 5-5, 5-6A, 5-6, 5-7, 8-7, 8-8, 8-9, 8-10, 9-4, 9-5, 9-6, 9-7, 10-8, 10-9, 11-1, 11-3, 11-4, 11-5, 11-6, 11-6B	9-1, 11-3, 11-4, 11-5, 11-6, 11-7, 11-8, Inv. 12-2
(8.7)(C)	9-4A, 9-4, 9-5A, 9-5	13-4, 13-5
Objective 8 The student will demonstrate an understanding of the concepts and uses of measurement and similarity.		
(8.8)(A)	Ch.11 Proj., 11-5A, 11-5, 11-6	12-5, 12-6
(8.8)(B)	Ch.11 Proj., 11-3, 11-4, 11-5, 11-6, 11-6B, Int. Inv. (pp. 556–557)	12-5, 12-6, 12-7, 12-8
(8.8)(C)	11-3, 11-4, 11-5, 11-6	12-5, 12-6, 12-7, 12-8
(8.9)(A)	9-4, 9-5, 9-6, 9-7	13-4, 13-5
(8.9)(B)	8-7, 8-8, 8-9	11-6, 12-8B
(8.10)(A)	1-8, 8-7, 8-10	3-5, 12-5, 14-4
(8.10)(B)	11-3, 11-4	12-8, 12-8B
Objective 9 The student will demonstrate an understanding of percents, proportional relationships, probability, and statistics in application problems.		
(8.1)(B)	3-3, 3-4, 3-5, 3-6A, 3-6, 7-1, 7-2, 7-3, 7-4, 7-7, 7-8, 7-9, 7-10, 8-1, 8-2, 8-3, 8-3B, 8-4, 8-5, 8-5B, 8-6, 8-7, 8-8, 8-8B, 8-9, 8-10, 11-7, 12-7A, 12-7	1-1, 1-6, 2-7, 3-1, 3-2, 3-4, 4-6, 4-8, 5-1, 6-1, 6-7, 7-5, 7-8, 8-4, 8-5, 8-6, 9-1, 9-5, 9-6, 9-7
(8.3)(B)	3-1, 3-2, 3-3, 3-4, 3-4B, 3-5, 3-6A, 3-6, 5-6, 7-5, 7-9, 8-1, 8-1B, 8-2, 8-3, 8-3B, 8-4, 8-5, 8-5B, 8-6, 8-7, 8-8, 8-9, 8-10, 12-7A, 12-7	4-5, 7-8, 8-4, 8-5, 8-6, 8-6B, 8-7, 9-1, 9-4, 9-5, 9-6, 9-8, 9-9, 9-10, 11-6, 11-7, Alt. Assmt. Inv.
(8.11)(A)	Ch.12 Proj., 12-5, 12-6A, 12-6	10-9, 10-10

Texas Assessment of Knowledge and Skills (TAKS)	Mathematics: Applications and Connections, Course 3	Pre-Algebra
(8.11)(B)	3-3, 6-6, Ch.12 Proj., 12-1A, 12-5, 12-6A, 12-6, 12-7A, 12-7, Ch.13 Proj.	9-3, 9-4B, 10-8, 10-8B, 12-3
(8.12)(A)	Ch.4 Proj., 4-4, 4-8	6-6, 10-2
(8.12)(C)	Ch.3 Proj., 3-6, Ch.4 Proj., 4-1, 4-1B, 4-2, 4-7, Ch.8 Proj., Ch.12 Proj.	1-10A, 1-10, 10-3B, 11-2
(8.13)(B)	4-8, 12-7	10-4
Objective 10 **The student will demonstrate an understanding of the mathematical processes and tools used in problem solving.**		
(8.14)(A)	1-1, 1-2, 1-3, 1-4, 1-5, 1-6, 1-7A, 1-7, 1-8, 1-9, 2-1, 2-2, 2-3, 2-4, 2-5, 2-6, 2-7, 2-8, 2-9, 2-9B, 2-10, 3-1, 3-2, 3-3, 3-4, 3-4B, 3-5, 3-6A, 3-6, Int. Inv. (pp. 136–137), 4-1A, 4-1, 4-2, 4-3, 4-3B, 4-4, 4-4B, 4-5, 4-5B, 4-6, 4-7, 4-8, 5-1, 5-2A, 5-2, 5-3, 5-4, 5-5, 5-6, 5-7, 6-1, 6-2, 6-2B, 6-3A, 6-3, 6-4, 6-5, 6-6, 6-7, 6-8, 6-9, Int. Inv. 9 pp. 274–275), 7-1, 7-2, 7-3, 7-4, 7-5A, 7-5, 7-5B, 7-6, 7-7, 7-8, 7-9, 7-10, 8-1, 8-1B, 8-2, 8-3, 8-3B, 8-4, 8-5, 8-5B, 8-6, 8-7, 8-8, 8-9, 8-10, 9-1, 9-2, 9-3, 9-4, 9-5A, 9-5, 9-6, 9-7, Int. Inv. (pp. 424–425), 10-1, 10-2, 10-3, 10-4A, 10-4, 10-5, 10-6A, 10-6, 10-7, 10-8, 10-9, 11-1, 11-2A, 11-2, 11-3, 11-4, 11-5, 11-6, 11-6B, 11-7, 12-1A, 12-1, 12-2, 12-3, 12-4, 12-5, 12-6A, 12-6, 12-7A, 12-7, Int. Inv. (pp. 556–557), 13-1, 13-2, 13-3, 13-4, 13-5, 13-6, 13-7A, 13-7	Every Lesson and Inv.
(8.14)(B)	1-1, 1-7A, 1-7, 2-7, 2-9, 2-9B, 3-6A, 3-6, 4-1A, 5-2A, 5-2, 5-3, 6-3A, 6-3, 6-8, 7-2, 7-3, 7-5A, 8-1, 8-3, 8-3B, 8-6, 9-5A, 10-6A, 10-7, 11-1, 11-2A, 11-5, 12-3, 12-4, 12-6A, 13-4, 13-7A, 13-7	1-1, 1-8, 2-4, 2-5, 2-7, 3-1, 3-6, 3-8, 4-1, 4-3, 5-7, 6-4, 6-8, 7-1, 7-3, 7-4, 7-7, 7-8, 8-5, 8-7, 9-4, 9-6, 10-5, 10-6, 10-8, 11-2, 11-6, 12-4, 12-5, 12-6, 12-7, 13-1, 13-4, 14-3, 14-4, 14-6
(8.14)(C)	1-1, 1-7A, 2-9A, 3-6A, 4-1A, 5-2A, 6-3A, 7-5A, 8-3B, 9-5A, 10-6A, 11-2A, 12-6A, 13-7A	1-1, 1-10A, 1-10, 2-1B, 2-4, 2-5, 2-6, 2-7, 3-1, 3-5, 3-6, 4-3, 4-7, 5-6, 5-7, 5-8, 6-4, 6-6, 6-8, 7-1, 7-3, 8-1, 8-4, 8-5, 9-2, 9-4, 9-6, 10-3, 10-5, 10-6, 10-8, 11-1, 11-1B, 12-2, 12-3, 12-4, 12-5, 13-2, 13-3, 13-5, 13-6, 13-6B, 13-7

Texas Assessment of Knowledge and Skills (TAKS)	Mathematics: Applications and Connections, Course 3	Pre-Algebra
(8.15)(A)	Ch.1 Proj., 1-1, 1-2, 1-3, 1-3B, 1-4, 1-5, 1-6, 1-7A, 1-7, 1-7B, 1-8, 1-9, Ch.2 Proj., 2-1, 2-2, 2-3, 2-4, 2-5, 2-6, 2-6B, 2-7, 2-8, 2-9A, 2-9, 2-9B, 2-10, Ch.3 Proj., 3-1, 3-2, 3-3, 3-4, 3-4B, 3-5, 3-6A, 3-6, Int. Inv. (pp. 136–137), Ch.4 Proj., 4-1A, 4-1, 4-1B, 4-2, 4-3, 4-3B, 4-4, 4-4B, 4-5, 4-5B, 4-6, 4-7, 4-8, Ch.5 Proj., 5-1A, 5-1, 5-1B, 5-2, 5-3A, 5-3, 5-4A, 5-4, 5-5, 5-5B, 5-6A, 5-6, 5-7, Ch.6 Proj., 6-1, 6-2, 6-2B, 6-3A, 6-3, 6-4, 6-5, 6-6, 6-7, 6-8A, 6-8, 6-9, Int. Inv. (pp. 274–275), Ch.7 Proj., 7-1, 7-2, 7-3, 7-4, 7-5A, 7-5, 75-B, 7-6, 7-6B, 7-7A, 7-7, 7-8, 7-9, 7-10, Ch.8 Proj., 8-1, 8-1B, 8-2, 8-3, 8-3B, 8-4, 8-5, 8-5B, 8-6, 8-7, 8-8, 8-8B, 8-9, 8-10, Ch.9 Proj., 9-1, 9-2A, 9-2, 9-3, 9-4A, 9-4, 9-5A, 9-5, 9-5B, 9-6, 9-7, Int. Inv. (pp. 424–425), Ch.10 Proj., 10-1, 10-1B, 10-2, 10-3, 10-4A, 10-4, 10-4B, 10-5, 10-6A, 10-6, 10-7, 10-8, 10-9, Ch.11 Proj., 11-1, 11-2A, 11-2, 11-3, 11-4, 11-5A, 11-5, 11-6, 11-6B, 11-7, Ch.12 Proj., 12-1A, 12-1, 12-2, 12-3, 12-4, 12-4B, 12-5, 12-6A, 12-6, 12-7A, 12-7, Int. Inv. (pp. 556–557), Ch.13 Proj., 13-1A, 13-1, 13-2, 13-3, 13-4, 13-5A, 13-5, 13-6, 13-7A, 13-7	Every Lesson and Inv.
(8.16)(A)	1-4, 1-5, 1-7, 1-7B, 1-8, 1-9, 2-3, 2-5, 2-7, 2-9A, 3-2, 3-4B, 4-3, 4-3B, 4-6, 5-1A, 5-1, 5-1B, 5-3, 5-4A, 5-4, 5-5B, 5-6A, 5-6, 5-7, 6-2, 6-2B, 6-7, 6-8A, 7-1, 7-3, 7-5B, 7-6, 7-6B, 7-7A, 8-4, 8-5, 8-7, 8-8B, 8-10, 9-2A, 9-3, 9-4A, 9-5B, 9-6, 9-7, 10-4A, 10-4, 10-5, 10-7, 10-8, 10-9, 11-3, 11-4, 11-5A, 11-5, 11-6, 11-6B, 12-1A, 12-2, 12-3, 12-4, 12-4B, 12-5, 12-6, 12-7A, 13-1A, 13-2, 13-3, 13-4, 13-5A, 13-5, 13-6, 13-7	1-10A, 2-1B, 3-1, 3-7, 4-1, 4-4B, 5-8, 8-1, 8-2, 8-6, 9-4B, 12-1A, 13-6A, 13-6
(8.16)(B)	1-1, 1-4, 1-5, 1-6, 1-7, 2-1, 2-2, 2-3, 2-4, 2-6B, 2-7, 2-8, 2-9, 2-9B, 2-10, 3-3, 3-5, 3-6, 4-1A, 4-1, 4-2, 4-3B, 4-4, 4-5B, 4-6, 4-7, 4-8, 5-1, 5-2, 5-3A, 5-3, 5-6, 6-1, 6-2, 6-3, 6-4, 6-5, 6-5, 6-8, 7-2, 7-3, 8-4, 7-5, 7-5B, 7-7A, 7-7, 7-8, 7-9, 8-1, 8-2, 8-3, 8-4, 8-5, 8-6, 8-7, 8-8B, 8-9, 8-10, 9-1, 9-3, 9-5, 9-6, 10-1, 10-1B, 10-3, 10-4A, 10-6, 10-7, 11-1, 11-3, 11-5, 11-6, 11-7, 12-1A, 12-2, 12-3, 12-4, 12-4B, 12-5, 12-6, 12-7, 13-1, 13-4, 13-6, 13-7A, 13-7	1-9, 3-7, 4-1, 4-4B, 5-8, 6-3, 6-5, 8-1, 8-2, 8-3, 8-4, 8-5, 8-6, 8-7, 8-8, 9-4, 9-4B, 9-10, 10-5, 10-6, 10-7, 10-8, 10-8B, 11-2, 12-1, 12-2, 12-3, 12-6, 12-7, 12-8

Name _____   Date _____

TAKS Practice
Objective 1A(b)(1)(A) _____

The student describes independent and dependent quantities in functional relationships.

Read each question and choose the best answer. Then write the letter for the answer you have chosen in the blank at the right of each question.

1 What is the independent variable in $y = 2x + 6$?

   A x

   B y

   C 6

   D 2

1 _____**A**_____

2 Nora runs around the track at a constant speed for several minutes. Which is the dependent quantity?

   A time Nora runs

   B Nora's speed

   C distance Nora runs

   D length of the track

2 _____**C**_____

3 What is the independent variable in $w = 17t - 50$?

   A 17

   B -50

   C w

   D t

3 _____**D**_____

4 The graph shows the resale value of a collectible stuffed bear that has been kept in perfect condition. What is the dependent quantity?

   A age of bear

   B resale value

   C original value

   D year of purchase

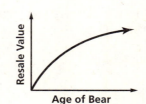

4 _____**B**_____

5 The formula $V = 4\pi r^2$ gives the volume V of a circular swimming pool 4 feet deep with radius r at Fair Park. What is the independent quantity?

   A radius of the pool

   B π

   C volume of the pool

   D depth of the water

5 _____**A**_____

TAKS Practice
Objective 1A(b)(1)(B)

The student uses data sets to determine functional (systematic) relationships between quantities.

Read each question and choose the best answer. Then write the letter for the answer you have chosen in the blank at the right of each question.

1 Isaac is driving from Austin to Amarillo. The following chart shows the number of miles he has traveled after each hour. Which of the following indicates the relationship between the number of hours h that he has traveled and the distance d traveled?

Hours	1	2	3	4	5
Distance (miles)	60	120	180	240	300

A $h = d + 60$ **B** $h = 60d$
C $d = h + 60$ **D** $d = 60h$

1 ___**D**___

2 Which of the following equations represents the relationship between Fahrenheit temperature F and Celsius temperature C according to the following data chart?

Celsius	0°	30°	100°
Fahrenheit	32°	86°	212°

A $F = 32 + \frac{9}{5}C$ **B** $F = C + 32$

C $C = \frac{5}{9}F - 32$ **D** $C = \frac{5}{9}(F + 32)$

2 ___**A**___

3 Which of the following functions contains these ordered pairs: $(1, -4)$, $(2, -5)$, $(3, -4)$, and $(4, -1)$?
A $f(x) = -x - 3$ **B** $f(x) = x^2 - 4x - 1$
C $f(x) = x^2 - 5$ **D** $f(x) = x^2 - 2x - 3$

3 ___**B**___

4 If a linear function contains the ordered pairs $(-10, 1)$, $(-4, 4)$, and $(2, 7)$, what will the value of the dependent variable be when the value of the independent variable is 8?

Record your answer and fill in the bubbles. Be sure to use the correct place value.

4

		1	0	.			
⓪	⓪	⓪	●		⓪	⓪	⓪
①	①	●	①		①	①	①
②	②	②	②		②	②	②
③	③	③	③		③	③	③
④	④	④	④		④	④	④
⑤	⑤	⑤	⑤		⑤	⑤	⑤
⑥	⑥	⑥	⑥		⑥	⑥	⑥
⑦	⑦	⑦	⑦		⑦	⑦	⑦
⑧	⑧	⑧	⑧		⑧	⑧	⑧
⑨	⑨	⑨	⑨		⑨	⑨	⑨

TAKS Practice
Objective 1A(b)(1)(C)

The student describes functional relationships for given problem situations and writes equations or inequalities to answer questions arising from the situations.

Read each question and choose the best answer. Then write the letter for the answer you have chosen in the blank at the right of each question.

1 Marie earns $4.50 per hour plus 3% commission for selling CDs. What is her total salary for a 40-hour week if she sells $4000 worth of CDs?

Record your answer and fill in the bubbles. Be sure to use the correct place value.

1

| 3 | 0 | 0 | . | | | |

2 Ian sells T-shirts and cowboy hats at the Texas State Fair. T-shirts cost $12 and hats cost $15. If Ian sells more than $500 in merchandise, he will win a coupon good for a one-day free admission to the amusement park. Let t be the number of T-shirts sold and h be the number of hats sold. Which inequality represents this situation?

A $t + h < 500$ **B** $t + h > 500$
C $12t + 15h < 500$ **D** $12t + 15h > 500$

2 _____ **D**

3 Which function gives the area A of a deck of uniform width x around a rectangular swimming pool 12 feet by 20 feet?

A $A = (20 - x)(12 + x)$
B $A = (20 + x)(12 + x)$
C $A = (20 + 2x)(12 + 2x) - 240$
D $A = (20 + 2x)(12 + x) - 240$

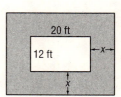

3 _____ **C**

4 Miguel is having shirts printed for everyone who attends a family reunion. There is a fixed cost of $25 for the design plus $8 per shirt. Which equation describes the cost c of printing n shirts?

A $c = 33n$ **B** $c = 8n + 25$
C $c = n + 8 + 25$ **D** $c = 25n + 8$

4 _____ **B**

TAKS Practice
Objective 1A(b)(1)(D)

The student represents relationships among quantities using models, tables, graphs, diagrams, verbal descriptions, equations, and inequalities.

Read each question and choose the best answer. Then write the letter for the answer you have chosen in the blank at the right of each question.

1 Which of the following situations could be represented by this graph?

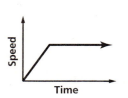

  A a car approaching a stop sign
  B a car leaving an expressway onto a local street
  C a car heading northeast, then turning east
  D a car starting from a stop sign, then speeding up until it reaches the speed limit on the street

1 ____**D**____

2 Sam walks three blocks at a certain speed, then gradually increases his speed to a run. He runs at a constant speed the rest of the way home. Which of the following graphs illustrates this situation?

2 ____**A**____

A

B

C

D
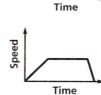

3 Which situation could be represented by the graph at the right?

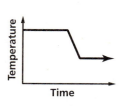

  A the temperature in a house in December before and after the heat is turned on
  B the temperature of a glass of milk when it is taken out of the refrigerator
  C the temperature in a house in July before and after the air conditioner is turned on
  D the temperature of a cup of coffee when it is heated

3 ____**C**____

TAKS Practice
Objective 1A(b)(1)(D) (continued)

Read each question and choose the best answer. Then write the letter for the answer you have chosen in the blank at the right of each question.

4 If the graph shows the function $f(x)$, what will $f(x)$ be when x is 7?

Record your answer and fill in the bubbles. Be sure to use the correct place value.

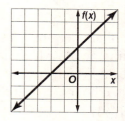

5 Which equation or inequality best represents the data in this chart?

5 ___**D**___

Cost of parking	$2.00	$4.00	$6.00
Hours in garage	less than 1	1 to 2	more than 2

A $C = 2h$
B $C < 2$
C $C > 2$
D $C \leq 2h$

6 Which situation would this graph most likely represent?

6 ___**C**___

A the number of mountains in Texas from 1975 to present
B the number of state capitals in Texas from 1975 to present
C the number of home computers owned by people in Texas from 1975 to present
D the number of typewriters in Texas from 1975 to present

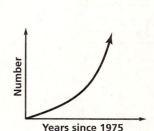

TAKS Practice
Objective 1A(b)(1)(E)

The student interprets and makes inferences from functional relationships.

Read each question and choose the best answer. Then write the letter for the answer you have chosen in the blank at the right of each question.

1 Teresa earns x dollars per hour at the local ice cream shop and time and a half for overtime hours, which are hours in addition to the normal 40 hours per week. Which equation gives her total salary t for a week in which she works h hours of overtime?

A $t = x + 1.5x(40)$

B $t = 40x + 1.5xh$

C $t = x + (h - 40)1.5$

D $t = 40x + 1.5(h - 40)$

1 ___**B**___

2 Tyler's total salary t at the department store is $6.00 per hour for stocking shelves 2 hours each day and $8.50 per hour for the remaining h hours he works. Which of the following functions gives his salary per day?

A $t = 6.00 + 8.50h$

B $t = 2(6.00 + 8.50h)$

C $t = 2(6.00) + 8.50h$

D $t = 2(6.00) + 8.50(h - 2)$

2 ___**C**___

3 Samantha works as a waitress. She earns $5.00 per hour plus 16% in tips. Tabitha works at a factory and earns $10.00 per hour. To earn the same amount in wages and tips as Tabitha earns in an 8-hour day, what must the total of the bills be at Samantha's tables?

A $31.25

B $40.00

C $250.00

D $500.00

3 ___**C**___

4 Brianna is on a diet. She plans to continue losing weight according to the pattern shown in the table. Predict her weight during the tenth week of her diet.

Week	1	2	3	4
Weight	150	148	146	144

Record your answer and fill in the bubbles. Be sure to use the correct place value.

4

1	3	2	.		
⓪	⓪	⓪	⓪	⓪	⓪	⓪
①	●	①	①	①	①	①
②	②	②	●	②	②	②
③	③	●	③	③	③	③
④	④	④	④	④	④	④
⑤	⑤	⑤	⑤	⑤	⑤	⑤
⑥	⑥	⑥	⑥	⑥	⑥	⑥
⑦	⑦	⑦	⑦	⑦	⑦	⑦
⑧	⑧	⑧	⑧	⑧	⑧	⑧
⑨	⑨	⑨	⑨	⑨	⑨	⑨

5 The function $f(x) = 9x + 4.50(x - 40)$ gives the total amount Siri earns when she works 40 hours or more in a week. How much does she earn in a 47-hour week?

A $391.50

B $423.00

C $454.50

D $634.50

5 ___**C**___

TAKS Practice
Objective 2A(b)(2)(A)

The student identifies the general forms of linear ($y = x$) and quadratic ($y = x^2$) parent functions.

Read each question and choose the best answer. Then write the letter for the answer you have chosen in the blank at the right of each question.

1 Which of these is a quadratic function?

   A $f(x) = 2$
   B $f(x) = 2x$
   C $f(x) = 2x^4$
   D $f(x) = 2x^2$

1   **D**

2 What value of a will make $f(x) = x^a + 2$ a linear function whose graph is not a horizontal line?

Record your answer and fill in the bubbles. Be sure to use the correct place value.

2

3 What type of function has a graph shaped like this?

   A increasing
   B linear
   C quadratic
   D decreasing

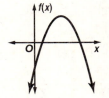

3   **C**

4 Which is a description of the graph of $y = x^2 + 6$?

   A a parabola that opens up and has a vertex at (0, 6)
   B a parabola that opens up and has a vertex at (6, 0)
   C a parabola that opens down and has a vertex at (0, 6)
   D a parabola that opens down and has a vertex at (6, 0)

4   **A**

5 Which is a description of the graph of $y = -5x$?

   A a line sloping up to the right
   B a line sloping up to the left
   C a horizontal line
   D a vertical line

5   **B**

TAKS Practice
Objective 2A(b)(2)(B) ————————————

For a variety of situations, the student identifies the mathematical domains and ranges and determines reasonable domain and range values for given situations.

Read each question and choose the best answer. Then write the letter for the answer you have chosen in the blank at the right of each question.

1 What is the domain of $f(x) = 2x - 6$?

  A all real numbers

  B all integers

  C $x \geq 0$

  D $y \geq -6$

1 ___**A**___

2 What is the range of $f(x) = x^2 - 4$?

  A all real numbers

  B all integers

  C $y \geq -4$

  D $x \geq 0$

2 ___**C**___

3 What is the domain of the function shown in this graph?

  A all real numbers

  B $x \neq 2$

  C $y > 0$

  D $y \neq 0$

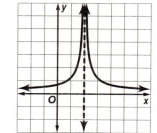

3 ___**B**___

4 What is the range of the function shown in this graph?

  A all real numbers

  B $-1 \leq x \leq 1$

  C $y \geq -1$

  D $-1 \leq y \leq 1$

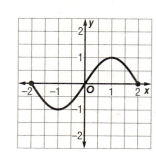

4 ___**D**___

TAKS Practice
Objective 2A(b)(2)(B) (continued)

Read each question and choose the best answer. Then write the letter for the answer you have chosen in the blank at the right of each question.

5 What value of x is not in the domain of $f(x) = \dfrac{1}{x-4}$?

Record your answer and fill in the bubbles. Be sure to use the correct place value.

5

			4	.			

⓪⓪⓪⓪   ⓪⓪⓪
①①①①   ①①①
②②②②   ②②②
③③③③   ③③③
④④④④④   ④④④
⑤⑤⑤⑤   ⑤⑤⑤
⑥⑥⑥⑥   ⑥⑥⑥
⑦⑦⑦⑦   ⑦⑦⑦
⑧⑧⑧⑧   ⑧⑧⑧
⑨⑨⑨⑨   ⑨⑨⑨

6 The function $c = 2.54x$ gives the number of centimeters c in a segment that is x inches long. What is a reasonable description of the domain of the function?

A $x \geq 2.54$

B $x < 2.54$

C $x < 1$

D $x > 0$

6 _____**D**_____

7 The function $y = 5x$ gives the value in cents of a set of x nickels. What is a reasonable range for the function?

A negative multiples of 5

B positive multiples of 5

C positive integers

D integers

7 _____**B**_____

8 A giant Ferris wheel in San Antonio has a diameter of about 100 feet. The bottom of the wheel is 4 feet above the ground. If $f(x)$ is a function that maps the time x Cindy rides on the Ferris wheel to her distance above the ground, what is a reasonable range for $f(x)$?

A all real numbers

B $y \leq 0$

C $4 \leq y \leq 104$

D $y \leq 100$

8 _____**C**_____

Name   Date

TAKS Practice
Objective 2A(b)(2)(C)

The student interprets situations in terms of given graphs.

Read each question and choose the best answer. Then write the letter for the answer you have chosen in the blank at the right of each question.

1 Which situation could be represented by this graph?

  A Mark is paid the same amount for each hour worked.

  B Mark is paid overtime when he works extra hours.

  C Mark works more hours in the morning than in the afternoon.

  D Mark works more hours in the afternoon than in the morning.

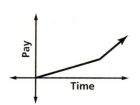

1   **B**

2 Which of the following graphs could be used to represent the height of a ball x seconds after it is thrown straight up into the air?

2   **A**

A
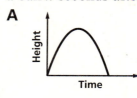

B
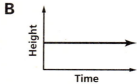

C
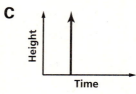

D
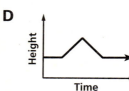

3 Which of the following is the graph of $y = 2$?

3   **D**

A
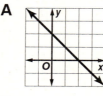

B
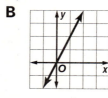

C
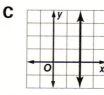

D
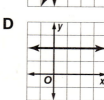

10   *TAKS Test Prep, Grade 9*

TAKS Practice
Objective 2A(b)(2)(C) (continued)

Read each question and choose the best answer. Then write the letter for the answer you have chosen in the blank at the right of each question.

4 The graph shows how the commission on the sale of a painting depends on the price of the painting. What is the commission rate expressed as a decimal?

Record your answer and fill in the bubbles. Be sure to use the correct place value.

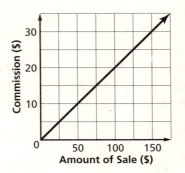

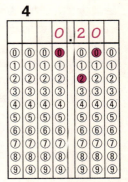

5 Which of the following graphs could represent the cost of *n* commemorative Davy Crockett 3-cent stamps?

5 _____**C**_____

A

B

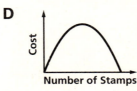

C

Cost / Number of Stamps

D

Cost / Number of Stamps

6 Which of the following functions is shown in this graph?

A $f(x) = 2x + 4$
B $f(x) = 2x^2 + 4$
C $f(x) = 2x^3 + 4$
D $f(x) = |2x + 4|$

6 _____**B**_____

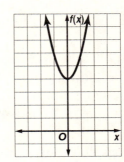

TAKS Practice
Objective 2A(b)(2)(D)

In solving problems, the student organizes data, interprets scatterplots, and models, predicts, and makes decisions and critical judgments.

Read each question and choose the best answer. Then write the letter for the answer you have chosen in the blank at the right of each question.

Use this stem-and-leaf plot for Questions 1–3. The numbers represent scores for students in a ninth-grade science class on a 50-point quiz.

Stem	Leaf
0	1 3 5
1	2 2 3 4
2	6 7 7 7 8

1 What does 1|3 represent in this stem-and-leaf plot?

Record your answer and fill in the bubbles. Be sure to use the correct place value.

1

2 How many students are in the science class?

A 3
B 9
C 12
D 15

2 ____ **C**

3 Which of the following would be a valid conclusion for the teacher to make based upon these quiz scores?

A Everyone understands the material very well.
B More than half the students understand the material very well.
C Several students do not understand the material well.
D None of the students understand the material well.

3 ____ **D**

4 Which relationship is shown by this scatterplot?

A As the cost goes down, the number sold goes down.
B As the cost goes up, the number sold goes down.
C As the cost goes down, the number sold remains constant.
D There is no relationship between cost and the number sold.

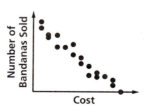

4 ____ **B**

TAKS Practice
Objective 2A(b)(2)(D) (continued)

Read each question and choose the best answer. Then write the letter for the answer you have chosen in the blank at the right of each question.

Use this box-and-whisker plot showing rodeo attendance for Questions 5–7.

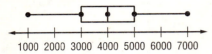

1000 2000 3000 4000 5000 6000 7000

5 What was the median attendance at the rodeo for one day?

  A 1000 people
  B 4000 people
  C 5000 people
  D 7000 people

5 ___**B**___

6 On what percent of the days was the attendance between 3000 and 4000 people?

  A 25%
  B 50%
  C 75%
  D 100%

6 ___**A**___

7 What was the highest attendance at the rodeo for one day?

  A 4000 people
  B 5000 people
  C 7000 people
  D 20,000 people

7 ___**C**___

8 This bar graph shows data from a survey about the three most popular movies in 2002. Approximately what percent of the people surveyed liked the movie *Lord of the Rings*?

  A 25%
  B 40%
  C 50%
  D 75%

8 ___**C**___

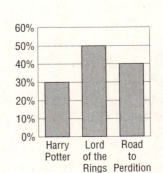

TAKS Practice
Objective 2A (b)(3)(A)

The student uses symbols to represent unknowns and variables.

Read each question and choose the best answer. Then write the letter for the answer you have chosen in the blank at the right of each question.

1 Which algebraic expression represents the sum of four times a number *n* and 9?

A $4 + n + 9$

B $n + 4(9)$

C $4n + 9$

D $4(n + 9)$

1 ____**C**____

2 Which equation says that six less than half a number *n* is 2?

A $6 - n = 2$

B $6 = \frac{1}{2}n - 2$

C $6 - \frac{1}{2}n = 2$

D $\frac{1}{2}n - 6 = 2$

2 ____**D**____

3 Which inequality could represent the situation that the number of longhorns ℓ is greater than twice the number of rattlesnakes *r*?

A $2\ell > r$

B $\ell > 2r$

C $\ell + 2r > 0$

D $2\ell + r < 0$

3 ____**B**____

4 If $2(x + k) + m$ represents twice the sum of a number *x* and 5, increased by 8, what is the value of *k*?

Record your answer and fill in the bubbles. Be sure to use the correct place value.

4

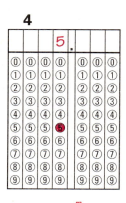

5 Which equation could represent the fact that the cost of a ticket to the Alamo Bowl has increased by $50 from $*x* to $*y*?

A $x + 50 = y$ **B** $x = y + 50$

C $50x = y$ **D** $x = 50y$

5 ____**A**____

Name _____ Date _____

TAKS Practice
Objective 2A(b)(3)(B)

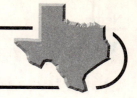

Given situations, the student looks for patterns and represents generalizations algebraically.

Read each question and choose the best answer. Then write the letter for the answer you have chosen in the blank at the right of each question.

1 Which expression represents the nth number in this pattern?

$-5, -3, -1, 1, 3, \ldots$

A $n - 6$ **B** $n + 2$

C $2n - 7$ **D** $2n + 2$

1 ___**C**___

2 What is the next number in the pattern?

$2, 11, 20, 29, 38, \ldots$

Record your answer and fill in the bubbles. Be sure to use the correct place value.

2

		4	7	.			
⓪	⓪	⓪	⓪		⓪	⓪	⓪
①	①	①	①		①	①	①
②	②	②	②		②	②	②
③	③	③	③		③	③	③
④	④	●	④		④	④	④
⑤	⑤	⑤	⑤		⑤	⑤	⑤
⑥	⑥	⑥	⑥		⑥	⑥	⑥
⑦	⑦	⑦	●		⑦	⑦	⑦
⑧	⑧	⑧	⑧		⑧	⑧	⑧
⑨	⑨	⑨	⑨		⑨	⑨	⑨

3 Fernando is arranging cans of corn on a grocery shelf as shown in this diagram. Each can of corn costs 59 cents. Which equation gives the number of cans c in each row, where n is the number of the row, beginning at the bottom, and n is between 1 and 7, inclusive?

row 3
row 2
row 1

A $c = 59n$ **B** $c = 6 - n$

C $c = 7 - n$ **D** $c = 8 - n$

3 ___**D**___

4 What is the sixth term in the sequence $2a - b, 5a - 2b, 8a - 3b, \ldots$?

A $20a - 7b$ **B** $17a - 6b$

C $14a - 5b$ **D** $11a - 4b$

4 ___**B**___

5 This chart shows the interest earned on savings accounts of different amounts. Which equation gives the interest i for one year if the original amount in the account is p dollars?

Amount	$50	$100	$250	$3000
Interest	$2.50	$5.00	$12.50	$150.00

A $i = 0.05p$ **B** $p = 0.05i$

C $i = 5p$ **D** $p = 5i$

5 ___**A**___

TAKS Practice
Objective 2A(b)(4)(A)

The student finds specific function values, simplifies polynomial expressions, transforms and solves equations, and factors as necessary in problem situations.

Read each question and choose the best answer. Then write the letter for the answer you have chosen in the blank at the right of each question.

1 Find $f(-1)$ if $f(x) = 3x^2 - 2x + 1$.

    A -4 **B** 0

    C 2 **D** 6

1 ____**D**____

2 Simplify $(2x - 7) + (-5x - 3)$.

    A $-3x - 10$ **B** $-3x - 4$

    C $-10x^2 + 21$ **D** $-10x^2 + 29x + 21$

2 ____**A**____

3 What is ℓ equal to in terms of P and w if $P = 2\ell + 2w$?

    A $\dfrac{P + 2w}{2}$ **B** $\dfrac{P - 2w}{2}$

    C $P + w$ **D** $P - w$

3 ____**B**____

4 What is the solution of $5x - 2 = 7x + 6$?

    A 2 **B** $\dfrac{1}{3}$

    C -4 **D** -2

4 ____**C**____

5 Factor $25x^2 - 49$.

    A $(5x + 7)^2$ **B** $(5x - 7)^2$

    C $(5x + 7)(5x - 7)$ **D** $25(x + 7)(x - 7)$

5 ____**C**____

6 For what value of a can $6x^2 - 11x - 35$ be factored as $(2x - 7)(3x + a)$?

Record your answer and fill in the bubbles. Be sure to use the correct place value.

6

			5	.			
⓪	⓪	⓪	⓪		⓪	⓪	⓪
①	①	①	①		①	①	①
②	②	②	②		②	②	②
③	③	③	③		③	③	③
④	④	④	④		④	④	④
⑤	⑤	⑤	●		⑤	⑤	⑤
⑥	⑥	⑥	⑥		⑥	⑥	⑥
⑦	⑦	⑦	⑦		⑦	⑦	⑦
⑧	⑧	⑧	⑧		⑧	⑧	⑧
⑨	⑨	⑨	⑨		⑨	⑨	⑨

TAKS Practice
Objective 2A(b)(4)(A) (continued)

Read each question and choose the best answer. Then write the letter for the answer you have chosen in the blank at the right of each question.

7 What are the solutions of $x^2 - 9x - 22 = 0$?

  A $-\frac{22}{9}, \frac{22}{9}$

  B $0, 9$

  C $2, -11$

  D $-2, 11$

7 _____**D**_____

8 The length of the sides of a triangular lot are consecutive even integers. If the perimeter of the lot is 384 feet, what is the length of the shortest side?

  A 125 ft

  B 126 ft

  C 127 ft

  D 128 ft

8 _____**B**_____

9 Maurice and Sergio went to the Aggies football game and spent $18.50 on h hot dogs and s sodas. Hot dogs cost $2.50 each and sodas cost $1.50 each. Which equation tells how h and s are related?

  A $h = 2.5$

  B $h = \frac{37 + 3s}{5}$

  C $h = \frac{37 - 3s}{5}$

  D $h = \frac{37}{5} - 1.5s$

9 _____**C**_____

10 The equation $h = 64t - 16t^2$ describes the height of a ball thrown directly upward with an initial velocity of 64 feet per second t seconds after it is thrown. How high above the ground does the ball travel?

  A 32 ft

  B 64 ft

  C 128 ft

  D 256 ft

10 _____**B**_____

TAKS Practice
Objective 2A(b)(4)(B)

The student uses the commutative, associative, and distributive properties to simplify algebraic expressions.

Read each question and choose the best answer. Then write the letter for the answer you have chosen in the blank at the right of each question.

1 Simplify $(5x^2 - 8x + 2) - (7x + 2x^2 - 5)$.

   A $3x^2 - 15x + 7$

   B $-2x^2 - 10x + 7$

   C $3x^2 - x - 3$

   D $7x^2 - 15x - 3$

1 ____**A**____

2 Which expression represents the area of a rectangle that has length $5x - 2$ and width $3x + 1$?

   A $8x - 1$

   B $16x - 2$

   C $15x^2 - 2$

   D $15x^2 - x - 2$

2 ____**D**____

3 Simplify $-4(2x - 6)$.

   A $-8x - 6$

   B $-8x - 24$

   C $-8x + 24$

   D $-6x + 24$

3 ____**C**____

4 Which expression requires you to use the Associative Property of Addition in order to simplify?

   A $[a + (-a)] + b$

   B $(a + b) + (-b)$

   C $a + [b + (-b)]$

   D $a + (-b + b)$

4 ____**B**____

5 When $12x^2y^3 + 48x^2y - 20x^3y^2$ is factored into $4x^2y(3y^2 + \underline{\quad} - 5xy)$ what number goes in the blank?

   Record your answer and fill in the bubbles. Be sure to use the correct place value.

5

			1	2	.			
⓪	⓪	⓪	⓪		⓪	⓪	⓪
①	①	❶	①		①	①	①
②	②	②	❷		②	②	②
③	③	③	③		③	③	③
④	④	④	④		④	④	④
⑤	⑤	⑤	⑤		⑤	⑤	⑤
⑥	⑥	⑥	⑥		⑥	⑥	⑥
⑦	⑦	⑦	⑦		⑦	⑦	⑦
⑧	⑧	⑧	⑧		⑧	⑧	⑧
⑨	⑨	⑨	⑨		⑨	⑨	⑨

TAKS Practice
Objective 3A(c)(1)(A)

The student determines whether or not given situations can be represented by linear functions.

Read each question and choose the best answer. Then write the letter for the answer you have chosen in the blank at the right of each question.

1 Which of the following situations could be represented by a linear function?

  A the area of a circle as a function of the radius

  B the distance traveled at 50 miles per hour as a function of time

  C the volume of a sphere as a function of the radius

  D the height of an object thrown directly upward as a function of time

1   **B**

2 Which linear function represents the interest I earned in one year if you invest p dollars at an interest rate of 3%?

  A $I = p^3$

  B $I = 3p$

  C $I = 0.03p$

  D $I = p + 0.03$

2   **C**

3 Tyson invited four hundred people to his wedding in Waco. The restaurant charges $42 per person plus $300 for the DJ. The total charge can be expressed as a linear function of the number of people attending. What is the slope of the graph of this linear function?

Record your answer and fill in the bubbles. Be sure to use the correct place value.

3

		4	2	.			
⓪	⓪	⓪	⓪		⓪	⓪	⓪
①	①	①	①		①	①	①
②	②	②	❷		②	②	②
③	③	③	③		③	③	③
④	④	❹	④		④	④	④
⑤	⑤	⑤	⑤		⑤	⑤	⑤
⑥	⑥	⑥	⑥		⑥	⑥	⑥
⑦	⑦	⑦	⑦		⑦	⑦	⑦
⑧	⑧	⑧	⑧		⑧	⑧	⑧
⑨	⑨	⑨	⑨		⑨	⑨	⑨

4 A company has been hired to paint the offices in a new building. Which statement is most likely to be true?

  A The number of gallons of paint needed is a linear function of the area to be painted.

  B The amount a painter earns per hour is a linear function of the area to be painted.

  C The number of gallons of paint needed is a linear function of the number of painters.

  D The number of painters is a linear function of the cost of the paint.

4   **A**

TAKS Practice
Objective 3A(c)(1)(C) ──────────────

The student translates among and uses algebraic, tabular, graphical, or verbal descriptions of linear functions.

Read each question and choose the best answer. Then write the letter for the answer you have chosen in the blank at the right of each question.

1 Which linear function describes the data in the table?

Height h (inches)	36	50	65
Weight w (pounds)	57	85	115

A $w = h + 35$
B $w = h + 21$
C $w = 2h - 15$
D $w = 2h - 78$

1 ___**C**___

2 What is the value of a for the linear function $f(x)$ described by the table?

Record your answer and fill in the bubbles. Be sure to use the correct place value.

x	$f(x)$
0	−2
1	0
5	a

2

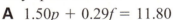

3 Ken and Louise are shopping for school supplies. Pens cost $1.50 each and folders cost $0.29 each. Which equation describes the situation if they spent $11.80?

A $1.50p + 0.29f = 11.80$
B $1.50p + 29f = 11.80$
C $p + f = 1.79$
D $p + f = 11.80$

3 ___**A**___

4 Which situation could be represented by this graph?

A There are 8 coins in a set of x nickels and y dimes.
B Linda is twice as old as her younger sister, and the sum of their ages is 8 years.
C Enrique lives twice as far from school as Andrea, and the distance between their homes is 8 miles.
D When asked to pick a decimal from 0 to 10, two students picked x, one picked y, and the total of all three choices was 8.

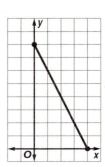

4 ___**D**___

TAKS Practice
Objective 3A(c)(1)(C) (continued)

Read each question and choose the best answer. Then write the letter for the answer you have chosen in the blank at the right of each question.

5 Which is the graph of $4x - 2y = 8$?

5 **B**

A
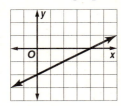

B
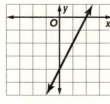

C
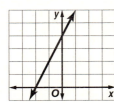

D
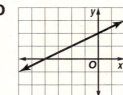

6 Ray spends twice as much time jogging as he does doing calisthenics. The total time he spends doing these two kinds of exercise is a function of the time he spends on calisthenics. Which is the graph of this function?

6 **C**

A
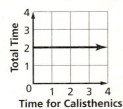

B
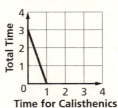

C
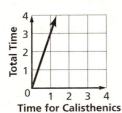

D
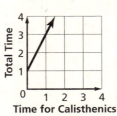

7 Ursula rides her motorcycle 5 miles every day from home to class at the local junior college. When she rides at 32 miles per hour, how many hours does the trip take her? Round your answer to 3 decimal places.

Record your answer and fill in the bubbles. Be sure to use the correct place value.

7

TAKS Practice
Objective 3A(c)(2)(A)

The student develops the concept of slope as rate of change and determines slopes from graphs, tables, and algebraic representations.

Read each question and choose the best answer. Then write the letter for the answer you have chosen in the blank at the right of each question.

1 What is the slope of the line shown in the graph?

   A 3

   B $\frac{1}{3}$

   C $-\frac{1}{3}$

   D -3

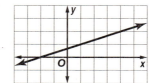

1   **B**

2 What is the slope of the line shown in the graph?

   A 2

   B $\frac{1}{2}$

   C 0

   D undefined slope

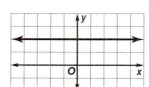

2   **C**

3 What is the slope of a flight of stairs if the width (tread) of each step is 8 inches and the height (rise) of each step is 6 inches, as shown in the diagram?

   A 2

   B -2

   C $\frac{4}{3}$

   D $\frac{3}{4}$

8 in.

6 in.

3   **D**

4 The cost of a trip over Spring Break to Padre Island is $7500 total for ten students from Denton High School. The per-student rate is the same for groups of any size. What is the slope of the graph of the linear function that gives the total cost for a group in terms of the number of students in the group?

Record your answer and fill in the bubbles. Be sure to use the correct place value.

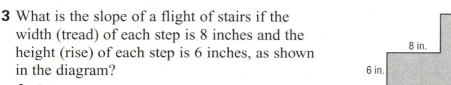

4

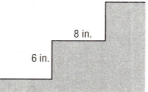

TAKS Practice
Objective 3A(c)(2)(A) (continued)

Read each question and choose the best answer. Then write the letter for the answer you have chosen in the blank at the right of each question.

5 The table gives information about how fast Mario was typing on the first day of a course for improving typing skills. At what rate was Mario typing on the first day?

5 __**C**__

Minutes	2	4	8
Number of Words Typed	100	200	400

A 200 words/min
B 100 words/min
C 50 words/min
D 25 words/min

6 What is the slope of the line whose equation is $5x - 3y = 15$?

6 __**A**__

A $\frac{5}{3}$
B $\frac{3}{5}$
C $-\frac{3}{5}$
D $-\frac{5}{3}$

7 An oil refinery purchases a new machine for $100,000. Each year the machine depreciates in value. What is the rate of change in the value of the machine if the depreciated value v of the machine t years after purchase is given by $v = 100,000 - 8000t$?

7 __**B**__

A $-$100,000/year
B $-$8000/year
C $8000/year
D $100,000/year

8 A college had 2800 students in 2000 and 3250 students in 2002. What is the rate of change in the number of students at this college per *year*?

8 __**A**__

A 225 students/year
B 450 students/year
C 550 students/year
D 1450 students/year

TAKS Practice
Objective 3A(c)(2)(B)

The student interprets the meaning of slope and intercepts in situations using data, symbolic representations, or graphs.

Read each question and choose the best answer. Then write the letter for the answer you have chosen in the blank at the right of each question.

1 The graph of a linear function has a y-intercept of 6. Which point must be on the graph?

A $(6, 0)$ **B** $(0, 6)$

C $(6, 6)$ **D** $(-6, 6)$

1 ___**B**___

2 What is the y-intercept of the graph of $3x - 4y = 20$?

A $\frac{20}{3}$ **B** 3

C -4 **D** -5

2 ___**D**___

3 If $y = 1.25x + 10$ is a function relating the cost y of printing x calendars for the South Rio Credit Union, what does the slope represent?

A $1.25 cost per calendar   **B** $10.00 cost per calendar

C $10.00 set up charge   **D** $1.25 set up charge

3 ___**A**___

4 A candy machine takes only dimes and nickels. It currently contains x nickels and y dimes, with a total value of $32. What does the x-intercept of the graph of $0.05x + 0.10y = 32$ tell you?

A the number of dimes if there are just as many dimes as nickels

B the number of nickels if there are 32 coins in all

C the number of nickels if there are no dimes

D the number of dimes if there are no nickels

4 ___**C**___

5 Which of these graphs has the greatest slope?

5 ___**D**___

A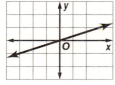

B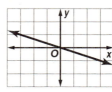

C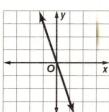

D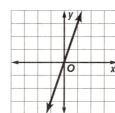

TAKS Practice

Objective 3A(c)(2)(B) (continued)

Read each question and choose the best answer. Then write the letter for the answer you have chosen in the blank at the right of each question.

6 Which of these graphs has the least *x*-intercept?

6 ___**D**___

A
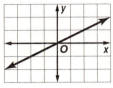

B
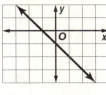

C
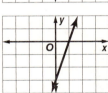

D
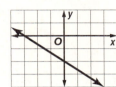

7 Rocky is hiking in Big Bend National Park. The path he is on rises in elevation 50 feet for each 10 minutes that he hikes. He starts his hike at an elevation of 1840 feet. His elevation *y* is a linear function of the number of minutes *x* he has hiked. What does the *y*-intercept of the function represent?

7 ___**C**___

A an elevation increase of 5 ft/min   **B** a rate of change of 0.2
C the beginning elevation   **D** the beginning time

8 What is the slope of side *AC* of this triangle? Round your answer to three decimal places.

Record your answer and fill in the bubbles. Be sure to use the correct place value.

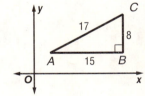

8

			0	.	5	3	3
⓪	⓪	⓪	⬤		⓪	⓪	⓪
①	①	①	①		①	①	①
②	②	②	②		②	②	②
③	③	③	③		③	⬤	⬤
④	④	④	④		④	④	④
⑤	⑤	⑤	⑤		⬤	⑤	⑤
⑥	⑥	⑥	⑥		⑥	⑥	⑥
⑦	⑦	⑦	⑦		⑦	⑦	⑦
⑧	⑧	⑧	⑧		⑧	⑧	⑧
⑨	⑨	⑨	⑨		⑨	⑨	⑨

9 If adult T-shirts cost \$15 and kids' T-shirts cost \$10, the equation $15x + 10y = 300$ describes the number of adult T-shirts *x* and kids' T-shirts *y* that can be bought for \$300. What does the *y*-intercept of the equation represent?

9 ___**C**___

A total cost of adult shirts
B total cost of kids' shirts
C number of kids' shirts if there are no adult shirts
D number of adult shirts if there are no kids' shirts

TAKS Practice
Objective 3A(c)(2)(C)

The student investigates, describes, and predicts the effects of changes in *m* and *b* on the graph of $y = mx + b$.

Read each question and choose the best answer. Then write the letter for the answer you have chosen in the blank at the right of each question.

1 The graph of $y = \frac{1}{2}x$ is shown at the right. If you were to slide the graph straight up 3 units, what would be an equation for the resulting graph?

   A $y = \frac{1}{2}x - 3$

   B $y = \frac{1}{2}x + 3$

   C $y + 3 = x$

   D $y - 3 = x$

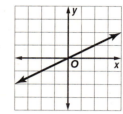

1   **B**

2 Suppose you graph $y = 5x - 4$. Which function can you graph to increase the *y*-intercept by 6 but leave the slope unchanged?

   A $y = 11x - 4$

   B $y = 11x + 2$

   C $y = 5x + 2$

   D $y = 5x - 10$

2   **C**

3 How are the graphs of $2x + 3y = 6$ and $2x + 3y = 3$ related?

   A parallel lines, *y*-intercepts differ by 1

   B parallel lines, *y*-intercepts differ by 3

   C slopes differ by 1

   D slopes differ by 3

3   **A**

TAKS Practice

Objective 3A(c)(2)(C) (continued)

Read each question and choose the best answer. Then write the letter for the answer you have chosen in the blank at the right of each question.

4 Each line graphed at the right has an equation of the form $y = mx - 2$. For which line is the value of m the least?

  A line a

  B line b

  C line c

  D line d

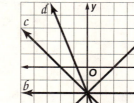

4   **D**

5 Denise graphed $y = 2x - 3$. Alberto multiplied the right side of the equation by 2 and graphed $y = 4x - 6$. Which is a true statement about the graphs?

  A The slopes are different, and so are the y-intercepts.

  B The slopes are the same, but the y-intercepts are different.

  C The slopes are different, but the y-intercepts are the same.

  D The slopes are the same, and so are the y-intercepts.

5   **A**

6 Suppose the graph of $y = \frac{5}{8}x + 7$ is moved straight to the right 1.85 units. What is the slope of the resulting line?

Record your answer and fill in the bubbles. Be sure to use the correct place value.

6

TAKS Practice
Objective 3A(c)(2)(D)

The student graphs and writes equations of lines given characteristics such as two points, a point and a slope, or a slope and *y*-intercept.

Read each question and choose the best answer. Then write the letter for the answer you have chosen in the blank at the right of each question.

1 The graph of $y = \frac{7}{8}x + b$ contains the point at (2, 3). What is the value of b?

Record your answer and fill in the bubbles. Be sure to use the correct place value.

1

				1	.	2	5
⓪	⓪	⓪	⓪		⓪	⓪	⓪
①	①	①	❶		①	①	①
②	②	②	②		❷	②	②
③	③	③	③		③	③	③
④	④	④	④		④	④	④
⑤	⑤	⑤	⑤		⑤	❺	⑤
⑥	⑥	⑥	⑥		⑥	⑥	⑥
⑦	⑦	⑦	⑦		⑦	⑦	⑦
⑧	⑧	⑧	⑧		⑧	⑧	⑧
⑨	⑨	⑨	⑨		⑨	⑨	⑨

2 Which is an equation of the line that has slope 5 and contains the point at (2, 3)?

A $y = 5x + 3$
B $y = 2x + 3$
C $y = 5x - 7$
D $y = 5x + 1$

2 ___**C**___

3 Which is an equation of the line that contains the points at (−3, 2) and (5, 6)?

A $y = \frac{1}{2}x + 2$

B $y = \frac{1}{2}x + \frac{7}{2}$

C $y = -2x - 4$
D $y = 2x + 8$

3 ___**B**___

4 Which is an equation of the line that has slope −3 and *y*-intercept 5?

A $y = \frac{1}{3}x + 5$

B $y = 3x + 2$
C $y = 5x - 3$
D $y = -3x + 5$

4 ___**D**___

5 Which is an equation of the line that has *y*-intercept 6 and *x*-intercept −2?

A $x - 3y = 6$
B $y = 3x + 6$
C $y = -2x + 6$
D $-2x + 6y = 1$

5 ___**B**___

TAKS Practice
Objective 3A(c)(2)(D) (continued)

Read each question and choose the best answer. Then write the letter for the answer you have chosen in the blank at the right of each question.

6 Which is an equation of the line that contains the point at $(-1, 6)$ and is perpendicular to the line $y = 4x - 2$?

6 ____**C**____

A $y = 4x + 10$

B $y = 4x - 25$

C $y = -\frac{1}{4}x + \frac{23}{4}$

D $y = -\frac{1}{4}x + \frac{25}{4}$

7 Which of the following is an equation of the line shown in the graph?

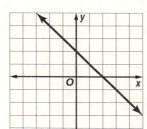

7 ____**D**____

A $y = 2$

B $y = 2x + 2$

C $y = x + 2$

D $y = -x + 2$

8 Which of these is an equation of the line that contains the points at $(7, 2)$ and $(7, -4)$?

8 ____**A**____

A $x = 7$

B $y = -2$

C $x = y - 6$

D $y = x - 5$

9 Which of these is an equation of the line that contains the points at $(7, -2)$ and $(5, -2)$?

9 ____**B**____

A $x = 7$

B $y = -2$

C $x = y - 2$

D $y = x - 9$

TAKS Practice
Objective 3A(c)(2)(E)

The student determines the intercepts of linear functions from graphs, tables, and algebraic representations.

Read each question and choose the best answer. Then write the letter for the answer you have chosen in the blank at the right of each question.

1 What is the x-intercept of the graph of $4x - 2y = 10$?

   A $\frac{5}{2}$

   B $\frac{2}{5}$

   C $-\frac{1}{5}$

   D -5

1   **A**

2 What is the y-intercept of the graph of $-3x - 12y = 9$?

   A -4

   B -3

   C $-\frac{4}{3}$

   D $-\frac{3}{4}$

2   **D**

3 The table shows data relating the number of first downs the Roughriders football team makes with the number of points they score in the game. Use a graphing calculator to find an equation for the line of best fit. What is the slope of the line? Write your answer rounded to three decimal places.

Number of first downs (x)	2	10	16
Points scored (y)	3	21	34

Record your answer and fill in the bubbles. Be sure to use the correct place value.

3

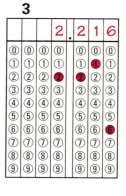

4 What is the x-intercept of the line shown in the graph?

   A 3

   B $\frac{4}{3}$

   C -4

   D -5

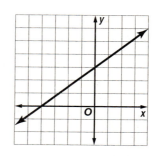

4   **C**

TAKS Practice
Objective 3A(c)(2)(E) (continued)

Read each question and choose the best answer. Then write the letter for the answer you have chosen in the blank at the right of each question.

5 What is the *x*-intercept of the graph of the linear function determined by the data in the table?

5 __**B**__

x	3	7	15
y	−1	−9	−25

A 5

B $\frac{5}{2}$

C 0

D −5

6 What is the *y*-intercept of the graph of the linear function determined by the data in the table?

6 __**A**__

x	−3	6	15
y	−1	5	11

A 1

B $\frac{2}{3}$

C 0

D −1

7 Use a graphing calculator to graph $y = 7.52x - 29.41$. What is the value of the *x*-intercept to the nearest tenth?

7 __**C**__

A −29.4

B 0.3

C 3.9

D 7.5

TAKS Practice
Objective 3A(c)(2)(F)

The student interprets and predicts the effects of changing slope and *y*-intercept in applied situations.

Read each question and choose the best answer. Then write the letter for the answer you have chosen in the blank at the right of each question.

1 The graph allows you to compare the costs of renting carpet cleaning equipment from four companies. Each company has a basic charge that all customers must pay. Additional charges are based on the hourly rate that each company charges for use of its equipment. Which company has the lowest hourly rate?

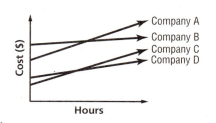

A company A
C company C
B company B
D company D

1 ___**B**___

2 The sum *S* of the measures of the interior angles of a regular polygon having *n* sides is given by the formula $S = (n - 2)180$. When the number of sides is increased by 1, what change takes place in the sum of the measures of the angles?

A It is multiplied by 180.
B It is decreased by 360.
C It is increased by 180.
D It is multiplied by 2.

2 ___**C**___

3 Rosita and Linda found that their monthly phone bills were linear functions of the number of minutes they used their phones. They graphed the functions to find out who pays more per minute. What information should they compare?

A the *y*-intercepts of the graphs
B the *x*-intercepts of the graphs
C the coordinates of the point where the graphs intersect
D the slopes of the graphs

3 ___**D**___

4 The velocity *v*, in feet per second, of a ball thrown straight up is described by $v = -32t + w$, where *t* is the time in seconds since the ball was released and *w* is velocity at the instant it was released. How will the graph of the function change if the ball is thrown faster?

A The slope will increase.
B The slope will decrease.
C The *y*-intercept will increase.
D The *y*-intercept will decrease.

4 ___**C**___

TAKS Practice

Objective 3A(c)(2)(F) (continued)

Read each question and choose the best answer. Then write the letter for the answer you have chosen in the blank at the right of each question.

5 The value of an antique vase was $700 in 1990. The value increased at the rate of $45 per year until 2000. From 2000 on, the value has increased $60 per year. What happens in the graph as you go from 1990 to the present time?

    A At 2000 the slope increases.

    B At 2000 the slope decreases.

    C At 2000 the y-intercept increases.

    D At 2000 the y-intercept decreases.

5 ___**A**___

6 Illinois has a state sales tax of 7.75%, while Texas has a state sales tax of 6.25%. If Juan bought a television set for $450 in Illinois and Linda bought the same type of television set in Texas, also for $450, how do the state sales taxes they each paid compare?

    A Juan paid $1.50 less than Linda.

    B Linda paid $1.50 less than Juan.

    C Juan paid $6.75 less than Linda.

    D Linda paid $6.75 less than Juan.

6 ___**D**___

7 Lula paid $5 for her fishing permit at Lake Fork. On Monday she caught x largemouth bass each weighing 10 pounds. The function $y = 10x + 2$ gives the total weight of the x fish plus her 2-pound bag to carry them in. On Tuesday she went back and caught x 13-pound bass but carried them in a net that only weighed $\frac{1}{2}$ pound. The function that gives the total weight of the fish and net is $y = 13x + \frac{1}{2}$. How did the slope and the y-intercept change from the first function to the second?

    A The slope increased by 3; the y-intercept decreased by $1\frac{1}{2}$.

    B The slope decreased by 3; the y-intercept increased by $1\frac{1}{2}$.

    C The slope increased by $1\frac{1}{2}$; the y-intercept decreased by 3.

    D The slope decreased by $1\frac{1}{2}$; the y-intercept increased by 3.

7 ___**A**___

TAKS Practice
Objective 3A(c)(2)(G)

The student relates direct variation to linear functions and solves problems involving proportional change.

Read each question and choose the best answer. Then write the letter for the answer you have chosen in the blank at the right of each question.

1 Johnson's Department Store marks clothes up 35% from their wholesale price to their selling price. How much would a coat sell for if the store paid $200 wholesale for it?

A $70   **B** $235

C $270   **D** $700

1 _____**C**_____

2 On December 29, 1998, Purdue played Kansas State in the Alamo Bowl. The attendance for the game was 60,780. If the ratio of Purdue fans to Kansas State fans was 2 to 5, approximately how many Kansas State fans were at the game?

A 43,414   **B** 36,468

C 24,312   **D** 17,366

2 _____**A**_____

3 The stopping distance for a car is directly proportional to the square of its speed. If the stopping distance for a car going 30 miles per hour is 75 feet, what is the stopping distance for a car going 60 miles per hour?

A 18.75 ft   **B** 150 ft

C 300 ft   **D** 37.5 ft

3 _____**C**_____

4 The volume of a sphere varies directly with the cube of its radius. If a sphere with radius 3 inches has volume 36π cubic inches, what is the volume of a sphere with radius 6 inches?

A 72π cu in.   **B** 108π cu in.

C 144π cu in.   **D** 288π cu in.

4 _____**D**_____

5 The cost of gasoline varies directly with the number of gallons purchased. If 10 gallons of gasoline cost $17.90, how much would 16 gallons cost?

Record your answer and fill in the bubbles. Be sure to use the correct place value.

5

	2	8	.	6	4	
⓪	⓪	⓪		⓪	⓪	⓪
①	①	①		①	①	①
②	●	②		②	②	②
③	③	③		③	③	③
④	④	④		④	●	④
⑤	⑤	⑤		⑤	⑤	⑤
⑥	⑥	⑥		●	⑥	⑥
⑦	⑦	⑦		⑦	⑦	⑦
⑧	⑧	●		⑧	⑧	⑧
⑨	⑨	⑨		⑨	⑨	⑨

TAKS Practice
Objective 4A(c)(3)(A)

The student analyzes situations involving linear functions and
formulates linear equations or inequalities to solve problems.

*Read each question and choose the best answer. Then write the
letter for the answer you have chosen in the blank at the right of
each question.*

1 During 1995 Princess Jewelers had sales of $42,000. During 1996 their
sales were $49,000. If the growth of sales is linear, which function
correctly relates sales s to the number of years t since 1995?

A $s = 7000t + 42,000$

B $s = 42,000t + 7000$

C $s - 42,000 = 7000(t - 1995)$

D $42,000s + 7000t = 1$

1 ____**A**____

2 Eleanor is landscaping her yard. She wants to buy bushes b that cost $19
each and perennial flower plants p that cost $6 each. She cannot spend
more than $200 on this landscaping project. Which linear inequality
could be used to find how many bushes and how many flower plants she
could afford?

A $b + p \leq 200$

B $19b \leq 200$ and $6p \leq 200$

C $19b + 6p \leq 200$

D $19b + 6p < 200$

2 ____**C**____

3 Which function could be used to find the expected Olympic winning
time for the men's 400-meter run in 2000, assuming that the relationship
is linear? Use the data in this table. Let s represent the winning time in
seconds and t represent the number of years after 1984.

Year	1984	1988	1992	1996
Winning time (seconds)	44.27	43.87	43.50	43.49

A $s = -0.1t + 44.27$

B $s = -0.07t + 178.61$

C $s = -0.27t + 44.19$

D $s = -0.07t + 44.19$

3 ____**D**____

Name _____ Date _____

TAKS Practice
Objective 4A(c)(3)(B) ————————————

The student investigates methods for solving linear equations and inequalities using models, graphs, and the properties of equality, selects a method, and solves the equations and inequalities.

Read each question and choose the best answer. Then write the letter for the answer you have chosen in the blank at the right of each question.

1 What is the solution of $4(x + 1) = 5x - 3$?

  A 7

  B 4

  C 1

  D -4

1 ___**A**___

2 What is the solution of $\frac{x + 3}{5} = \frac{3x - 6}{3}$?

Record your answer and fill in the bubbles. Be sure to use the correct place value.

2

3 What is the solution of $-8 \leq 3 - 2(x + 6)$?

  A $x \geq \frac{23}{2}$ **B** $x \geq \frac{5}{2}$

  C $x \leq -\frac{1}{2}$ **D** $x \leq \frac{17}{2}$

3 ___**C**___

4 What is the solution of $7 - 3x = 4x + 2 - 7x$?

  A 0   **B** $\frac{5}{14}$

  C $\frac{5}{7}$ **D** no solution

4 ___**D**___

5 To solve $5x + 1 = 16$ on his graphing calculator, Obi can graph $y = 5x + 1$ and find where the graph intersects the graph of which of the following equations?

  A $y = 16x + 1$

  B $y = 5x + 16$

  C $x = 16$

  D $y = 16$

5 ___**D**___

Answer grid: 3.25

TAKS Practice
Objective 4A(c)(3)(B) (continued)

Read each question and choose the best answer. Then write the letter for the answer you have chosen in the blank at the right of each question.

6 Zander can win the Mathlete meet if he correctly solves the inequality $2 < 3x - 1 < 4$. Which of the following compound inequalities should Zander solve?

A $3x - 1 > 2$ or $3x - 1 < 4$

B $3x - 1 > 2$ and $3x - 1 < 4$

C $3x - 1 < 2$ or $3x - 1 < 4$

D $3x - 1 < 2$ and $3x - 1 < 4$

6 ___**B**___

7 Which graph shows the solutions of $3x + 2y \geq 6$?

7 ___**C**___

A
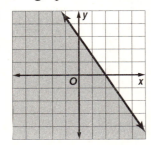

B
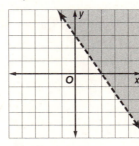

C
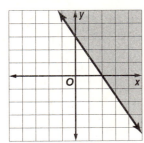

D
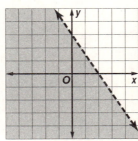

8 Ledd Corporation produces a CD-RW drive at a cost of $120 each with fixed costs of $36,000. The CD-RW drive sells for $180. How many drives must Ledd Corporation sell to break even (cover their expenses)?

A 600

B 300

C 200

D 60

8 ___**A**___

TAKS Practice
Objective 4A(c)(3)(C)

For given contexts, the student interprets and determines the
reasonableness of solutions to linear equations and inequalities.

*Read each question and choose the best answer. Then write the
letter for the answer you have chosen in the blank at the right of
each question.*

1 An adult ticket at the puppet theater costs \$20. The equation $y = 20x$
describes total adult ticket sales y for one day in terms of the number of
adult tickets x that the theater sells. Which is a reasonable solution for
the equation in this situation?

  A (20, 1)

  B (20, 400)

  C (400, 20)

  D (0.5, 10)

1 ___**B**___

2 A picture frame for Juanita's class photo is to have a perimeter of
18 inches. If the width of the frame is x inches and the length is y inches,
then $2x + 2y = 18$. Which solution of this equation is the most
reasonable when she selects a frame?

  A (3, 6)

  B (1, 8)

  C (8, 1)

  D (18, 0)

2 ___**A**___

3 The number of chirps C that a particular type of cricket makes per
minute can be used to estimate the temperature T in degrees Fahrenheit.
The formula for T in terms of C is $T = \frac{1}{4}C + 37$. Which of the
following is a reasonable value you might use for C in this situation?

  A -5

  B 20.5

  C 74

  D 100

3 ___**B**___

4 Jebb has x nickels and y dimes, and their total value is less than 90 cents.
The ordered pairs that he might have are described by $5x + 10y < 90$.
Which ordered pair shows a coin combination he might have?

  A $(-2, 8)$

  B $(8, -2)$

  C $(5, 5)$

  D $\left(10, \frac{1}{2}\right)$

4 ___**C**___

TAKS Practice
Objective 4A(c)(4)(A)

The student analyzes situations and formulates systems of linear equations to solve problems.

Read each question and choose the best answer. Then write the letter for the answer you have chosen in the blank at the right of each question.

1 Marianna has a collection of n nickels and d dimes. She has 3 more nickels than dimes, and the total value of the collection is \$1.20. Which system would you solve to find the number of coins of each type in her collection?

A $n + d = 120$
  $n - d = 3$

B $n - d = 3$
  $5n + 10d = 1.20$

C $n - d = 3$
  $5n + 10d = 120$

D $d = 2n$
  $n - d = 3$

1 ____**C**____

2 The Wheatfield restaurant has t tables that seat 4 people each and b booths that seat 6 people each. The restaurant can seat 200 people in its total of 42 seating units. Which system of equations could you solve to find the number of tables and the number of booths?

A $t + b = 42$
  $4t + 6b = 200$

B $t + b = 200$
  $4t + 6b = 42$

C $4t = 200$
  $6b = 200$

D $4t + 6b = 42$
  $4t + 6b = 200$

2 ____**A**____

3 Ruba went boating on the Medina River. If the boat went 20 miles in 2 hours downstream and returned the 20 miles upstream in $2\frac{1}{2}$ hours, what was the speed of the current in miles per hour?

Record your answer and fill in the bubbles. Be sure to use the correct place value.

3

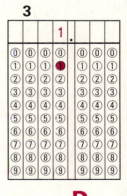

4 Which would be a good first step to use to solve this system?
  $y = 6x + 4$
  $5x + 2y = 12$

A Multiply the first equation by 2, and add the result to the second equation.

B Substitute $\frac{1}{6}y - 4$ for x in the second equation.

C Substitute $6x + 4$ for x in the second equation.

D Substitute $6x + 4$ for y in the second equation.

4 ____**D**____

TAKS Practice

Objective 4A(c)(4)(A) (continued)

Read each question and choose the best answer. Then write the letter for the answer you have chosen in the blank at the right of each question.

5 Which might be your first step if you want to solve the system by elimination?

$5x + 10y = 7$
$2x - 6y = 3$

A Substitute $-10y + 7$ for x in the second equation.

B Substitute $3y + 3$ for x in the second equation.

C Multiply the first equation by 3, multiply the second equation by 5, then add the resulting equations together.

D Multiply the first equation by 2, multiply the second equation by 5, then add the resulting equations together.

5 ___**C**___

6 Westlake Catalog sells Mavericks jerseys for $39 and Rangers hats for $18. Megan orders j jerseys and h hats. The total number of items is 25, and the total cost is $702. Which system of equations could you solve to find how many of each item she ordered?

A $j = 39$
$h = 18$

B $j + h = 25$
$j + h = 702$

C $j + h = 25$
$39j + 18h = 702$

D $j + h = 702$
$39j + 18h = 25$

6 ___**C**___

7 Roy is twice as old as Gene. In 15 years Roy will be 9 years older than Gene will be. How old is Roy now?

A 9

B 18

C 24

D 33

7 ___**B**___

8 The sum of two numbers is 18. The difference of the numbers is 8. Which is the greater of the two numbers?

A 13

B 10

C 9

D 5

8 ___**A**___

TAKS Practice
Objective 5A(d)(1)(C)

The student investigates, describes, and predicts the effects of changes in c on the graph of $y = x^2 + c$.

Read each question and choose the best answer. Then write the letter for the answer you have chosen in the blank at the right of each question.

1 Which of the following is the graph of $y = x^2 + 2$?

1 ____**B**____

A
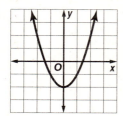

B
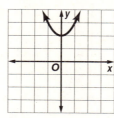

C
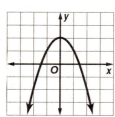

D
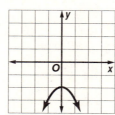

2 How can the graph of $y = x^2 - 12$ be obtained from the graph of $y = x^2$?

2 ____**A**____

  A Move the graph of $y = x^2$ down 12.
  B Move the graph of $y = x^2$ up 12.
  C Move the graph of $y = x^2$ right 12.
  D Move the graph of $y = x^2$ left 12.

3 How can the graph of $y = -x^2$ be obtained from the graph of $y = x^2$?

3 ____**B**____

  A Reflect the graph of $y = x^2$ over the y-axis.
  B Reflect the graph of $y = x^2$ over the x-axis.
  C Reflect the graph of $y = x^2$ over the line $y = x$.
  D Reflect the graph of $y = x^2$ over the line $y = -x$.

4 How can the graph of $y = x^2 + 6$ be obtained from the graph of $y = x^2 - 8$?

4 ____**D**____

  A Move the graph of $y = x^2 - 8$ up 6.
  B Move the graph of $y = x^2 - 8$ down 8.
  C Move the graph of $y = x^2 - 8$ down 14.
  D Move the graph of $y = x^2 - 8$ up 14.

TAKS Practice

Objective 5A(d)(1)(C) (continued) ─────────────

Read each question and choose the best answer. Then write the letter for the answer you have chosen in the blank at the right of each question.

5 This graph shows an equation in the form $y = x^2 + c$. What is the value of c?

Record your answer and fill in the bubbles. Be sure to use the correct place value.

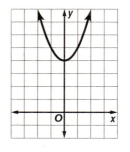

5

6 Which of the following is the graph of $y = x^2 - 3$?   **6** ___**C**___

A
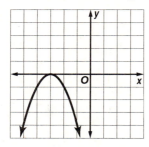

B
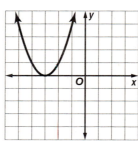

C
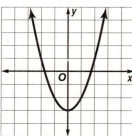

D
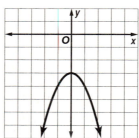

7 How is the graph of $y = x^2 + 2c$ related to the graph of $y = x^2 + c$ if   **7** ___**D**___
c is a positive number?

  A It is 2 units higher in the coordinate plane.
  B It is 2 units lower in the coordinate plane.
  C It is c units lower in the coordinate plane.
  D It is c units higher in the coordinate plane.

TAKS Practice
Objective 5A(d)(3)(A)

The student uses the laws of exponents and applies them in problem-solving situations.

Read each question and choose the best answer. Then write the letter for the answer you have chosen in the blank at the right of each question.

1 Olga saves 1 penny on January 1, 2 pennies on January 2, 4 pennies on January 3, and so on. If this pattern continues, how many pennies does she save on January 12?

  A 4096

  B 2048

  C 12

  D 400

1 ____**B**____

2 Paul bought a car for \$35,000. If the car depreciates at 20% per year, how much will it be worth in 6 years? Use the formula $D = C(1 - r)^t$, where D is the depreciated value, C is the original value, r is the rate of depreciation, and t is the time (in years) over which the depreciation occurs. Write your answer rounded to the nearest dollar.

Record your answer and fill in the bubbles. Be sure to use the correct place value.

3 What is the area of this triangle expressed in terms of x?

  A $12x^3$

  B $24x^3$

  C $12x^2$

  D $2x^2 + 12x$

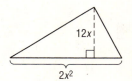

3 ____**A**____

4 The half-life of a radioactive substance is the length of time it takes for half of it to change to a different substance. If the half-life of a substance is 6 hours, how much of a 100-gram sample will be left after 24 hours?

  A 25 g

  B 16.6 g

  C 12.5 g

  D 6.25 g

4 ____**D**____

TAKS Practice
Objective 6(8.6)(A)

The student is expected to generate similar shapes using dilations including enlargements and reductions.

Read each question and choose the best answer. Then write the letter for the answer you have chosen in the blank at the right of each question.

1 Which of the following shows the side lengths of the triangle at the right after a dilation with scale factor $\frac{1}{2}$?

A

B

C

D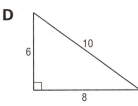

1 ___**A**___

2 Which figure is similar to the rectangle shown at the right?

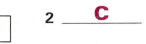

A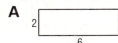

B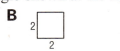

C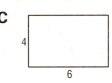

D

2 ___**C**___

3 Which pair of shapes appear similar?

A

B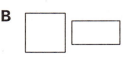

C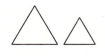

D

3 ___**C**___

TAKS Practice
Objective 6(8.6)(A) (continued)

Read each question and choose the best answer. Then write the letter for the answer you have chosen in the blank at the right of each question.

4 Which shape is similar to the given shape?

A

B

C

D

4 _____**B**_____

5 A photograph of the stars of the television series *Dallas* is 2 inches wide and 3 inches long. If an enlargement is to have a width of 8 inches, what will the length be?

Record your answer and fill in the bubbles. Be sure to use the correct place value.

5

		1	2	.			
⓪	⓪	⓪	①		⓪	⓪	⓪
①	①	●	①		①	①	①
②	②	②	●		②	②	②
③	③	③	③		③	③	③
④	④	④	④		④	④	④
⑤	⑤	⑤	⑤		⑤	⑤	⑤
⑥	⑥	⑥	⑥		⑥	⑥	⑥
⑦	⑦	⑦	⑦		⑦	⑦	⑦
⑧	⑧	⑧	⑧		⑧	⑧	⑧
⑨	⑨	⑨	⑨		⑨	⑨	⑨

6 If these two rectangles are similar, what is the value of *x*?

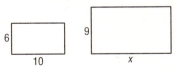

6 _____**A**_____

A 15
B 10
C 8
D 5

TAKS Practice
Objective 6(8.6)(B)

The student is expected to graph dilations, reflections, and translations on a coordinate plane.

Read each question and choose the best answer. Then write the letter for the answer you have chosen in the blank at the right of each question.

1 Which of the following is the graph of the reflection of △*ABC* over the line *y* = 2?

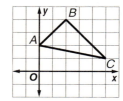

1 _____**C**_____

A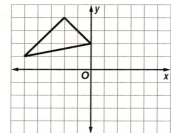

B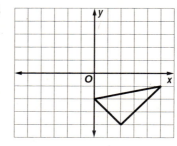

C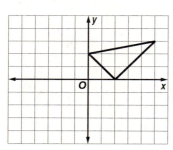

D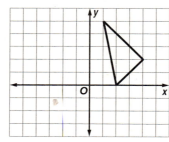

2 Suppose △*ABC* is dilated using the scale factor 3 and the origin as center. What are the coodinates of the image of point *A*?

A (4, 8)
B (18, 6)
C (9, −9)
D (3, 15)

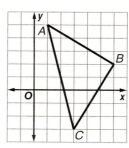

2 _____**D**_____

3 A translation maps (*x*, *y*) onto (*x* + 4, *y* − 6). What is the image of (−5, 2) for this transformation?

A (−1, −4)
B (9, −8)
C (−9, 8)
D (1, 4)

3 _____**A**_____

TAKS Practice

Objective 6(8.6)(B) (continued)

Read each question and choose the best answer. Then write the letter for the answer you have chosen in the blank at the right of each question.

4 The image of $(3, -9)$ under a dilation with scale factor $\frac{1}{3}$ and center $(0, 0)$ is $(a, -3)$. What is the value of a?

Record your answer and fill in the bubbles. Be sure to use the correct place value.

4

1	.		

⓪	⓪	⓪	⓪		⓪	⓪	⓪
①	①	①	●		①	①	①
②	②	②	②		②	②	②
③	③	③	③		③	③	③
④	④	④	④		④	④	④
⑤	⑤	⑤	⑤		⑤	⑤	⑤
⑥	⑥	⑥	⑥		⑥	⑥	⑥
⑦	⑦	⑦	⑦		⑦	⑦	⑦
⑧	⑧	⑧	⑧		⑧	⑧	⑧
⑨	⑨	⑨	⑨		⑨	⑨	⑨

5 What is the length of the image of $\overline{AB}$ under an enlargement of magnitude 4 where A has coordinates $(6, -1)$ and B has coordinates $(2, 0)$?

A $\sqrt{17}$

B $4\sqrt{37}$

C $4\sqrt{17}$

D $3\sqrt{37}$

5 **C**

6 The graph of $\triangle ABC$ with $A(1, 2)$, $B(2, 4)$, and $C(3, -2)$ is reflected over the y-axis and then translated 4 units to the right. What are the coordinates of the image of A?

A $(3, 2)$

B $(5, -2)$

C $(3, -2)$

D $(5, 2)$

6  **A**

7 $A(1, 0)$, $B(2, 3)$, and $C(4, 1)$ are the vertices of $\triangle ABC$. Suppose $\triangle ABC$ is reflected over the x-axis and that the image is translated 2 units down. What are the coordinates of the image of point A?

A $(1, -2)$

B $(0, 1)$

C $(1, -3)$

D $(-1, 2)$

7 _____ **A**

TAKS Practice
Objective 6(8.7)(D)

The student is expected to locate and name points on a coordinate plane using ordered pairs of rational numbers.

Read each question and choose the best answer. Then write the letter for the answer you have chosen in the blank at the right of each question.

1 What is the *x*-coordinate of point *P*?

Record your answer and fill in the bubbles. Be sure to use the correct place value.

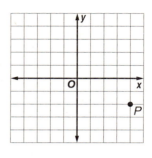

1

2 What are the coordinates of point *Q*?

  A (4, 3)
  B (3, 4)
  C (3, −4)
  D (−3, 4)

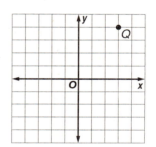

2 _____ **B**

3 Which point is below the *x*-axis and to the right of the *y*-axis?

  A (−2, −1)   **B** (−2, 1)
  C (−1, 2)   **D** (1, −2)

3 _____ **D**

4 Which point has coordinates (−3, 4)?

  A *A*
  B *B*
  C *C*
  D *D*

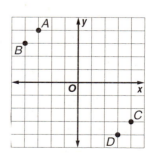

4 _____ **A**

5 Which point is in Quadrant III?

  A (−2, 1)   **B** (3, −4)
  C (−1, −6)   **D** (2, 8)

5 _____ **C**

TAKS Practice
Objective 7(8.7)(A)

The student draws solids from different perspectives.

Read each question and choose the best answer. Then write the letter for the answer you have chosen in the blank at the right of each question.

1 What kind of figure is shown in the diagram?

   A a rectangular prism

   B a triangular prism

   C a rectangular pyramid

   D a triangular pyramid

1   **B**

2 What kind of figure is shown in the diagram?

   A a sphere

   B a cone

   C a prism

   D a cylinder

2   **D**

3 Which of the following could be the shape of a horizontal cross section of the figure shown at the right?

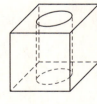

3   **C**

   A

   B

   C

   D

4 Which of the following could be the shape of a vertical cross section of the figure shown at the right?

4   **B**

   A

   B

   C

   D

TAKS Practice
Objective 7(8.7)(A) (continued)

Read each question and choose the best answer. Then write the letter for the answer you have chosen in the blank at the right of each question.

5 What figure is formed when the rectangle shown at the right is rotated about the dashed vertical line?

5 ___**C**___

A

B

C

D

6 Which figure is the same as the figure at the right, but in a different position?

6 ___**A**___

A

B

C

D

7 When this pattern is folded into a cylinder, what will the height of the cylinder be?

Record your answer and fill in the bubbles. Be sure to use the correct place value.

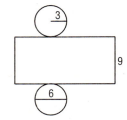

7

			9	.			
⓪	⓪	⓪	⓪		⓪	⓪	⓪
①	①	①	①		①	①	①
②	②	②	②		②	②	②
③	③	③	③		③	③	③
④	④	④	④		④	④	④
⑤	⑤	⑤	⑤		⑤	⑤	⑤
⑥	⑥	⑥	⑥		⑥	⑥	⑥
⑦	⑦	⑦	⑦		⑦	⑦	⑦
⑧	⑧	⑧	⑧		⑧	⑧	⑧
⑨	⑨	⑨	●		⑨	⑨	⑨

TAKS Practice
Objective 7(8.7)(B)

The student is expected to use geometric concepts and properties to solve problems in fields such as art and architecture.

Read each question and choose the best answer. Then write the letter for the answer you have chosen in the blank at the right of each question.

1 What is the area of the Norman window shown in the diagram?

A $32 + 2\pi$
B $32 + 4\pi$
C $16 + 2\pi$
D $16 + 4\pi$

1 ___**A**___

2 A zoo entrance is an arch with the shape of the parabola $y = -x^2 + 16$, where x and y are measured in feet. Approximately how wide is the archway across the bottom?

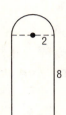

A 16 ft
B 12 ft
C 8 ft
D 4 ft

2 ___**C**___

3 A dance floor has hexagonal tiles, as shown in the diagram. If the sides of each tile are 8 inches long, what is the width x of each tile?

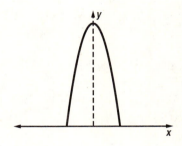

A 24 in.
B 16 in.
C 18 in.
D 83 in.

3 ___**B**___

4 Garfield built a rectangular treehouse for his children. He wants to paint the outside, including the top and bottom. If one gallon of paint covers 400 square feet and he needs to put on two coats of paint, how many gallons of paint must he buy? He cannot buy partial gallons.

A 1 gal
B 2 gal
C 4 gal
D 8 gal

4 ___**B**___

Read each question and choose the best answer. Then write the letter for the answer you have chosen in the blank at the right of each question.

5 The diagram shows a scale drawing of Irena's bedroom. If 1 inch in the drawing represents $\frac{1}{2}$ foot in the actual bedroom, what is the length of the long wall of the bedroom?

Record your answer and fill in the bubbles. Be sure to use the correct place value.

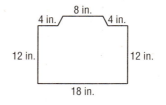

6 A carpenter is building a roof that is 42 feet across at the base, as shown in the diagram. The roof has a pitch of 8 inches for every foot of length along the base. What is the length x of the roof support needed at the highest point of the roof?

42 ft

A 168 ft
B 28 ft
C 14 ft
D 7 ft

6 _____ **C** _____

7 The doorway between Ricky's living room and dining room is shaped as shown in the diagram. Approximately how many feet long is x?

A 3.5 ft
B 3 ft
C 2 ft
D 1.4 ft

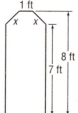

7 _____ **D** _____

TAKS Practice
Objective 7(8.7)(C) ——————————————

The student is expected to use pictures or models to demonstrate the Pythagorean Theorem.

Read each question and choose the best answer. Then write the letter for the answer you have chosen in the blank at the right of each question.

1 According to the Pythagorean Theorem, which equation must be true?

A $a^2 + c^2 = b^2$
B $a^2 + b^2 = c^2$
C $b^2 + c^2 = a^2$
D $a^2 = b^2$

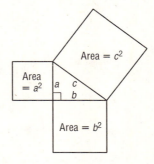

1 ___**B**___

2 Each right triangle in the diagram below is congruent to the right triangle shown at the right. The area of the entire large square is c^2. What other expression gives the area of the large square?

2 ___**C**___

A $4\left(\dfrac{ab}{2}\right)$

B $ab + 4abc$

C $(a - b)^2 + 4\left(\dfrac{ab}{2}\right)$

D $(a + b)^2 + 4\left(\dfrac{ab}{2}\right)$

3 What is the value of x in this right triangle?

A $\sqrt{17}$
B $\sqrt{119}$
C 11
D 13

3 ___**D**___

4 How long is the diagonal of the box shown in this diagram?

A 26
B 38
C 42
D 124

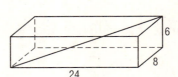

4 ___**A**___

TAKS Practice
Objective 7(8.7)(C) (continued)

Read each question and choose the best answer. Then write the letter for the answer you have chosen in the blank at the right of each question.

5 What is the value of *x* in this right triangle?

Record your answer and fill in the bubbles. Be sure to use the correct place value.

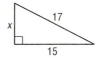

6 A triangle has side lengths 7 centimeters, 12 centimeters, and 16 centimeters. Which statement can you use to convince someone that the triangle is not a right triangle?

A $16 < 7 + 12$

B $7^2 + 16^2 > 12^2$

C $12^2 + 16^2 > 7^2$

D $7^2 + 12^2 < 16^2$

6 ____**D**____

7 Which triangle is a right triangle?

A
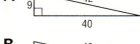

B

C
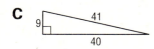

D

7 ____**C**____

8 What is the length *x* of the diagonal of the rectangle?

A 6

B $\sqrt{41}$

C $\sqrt{51}$

D 9

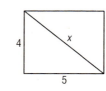

8 ____**B**____

TAKS Practice
Objective 8(8.8)(A)

The student is expected to find surface area of prisms and cylinders using models and nets.

Read each question and choose the best answer. Then write the letter for the answer you have chosen in the blank at the right of each question.

1 What is the surface area of the rectangular prism?

   A 320 cm²

   B 184 cm²

   C 92 cm²

   D 72 cm²

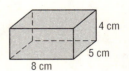

1   **B**

2 What is the surface area of the cube?

Record your answer and fill in the bubbles. Be sure to use the correct place value.

2

1 5 0 .

3 What is the surface area of the cylinder?

   A 336π ft²

   B 196π ft²

   C 128π ft²

   D 40π ft²

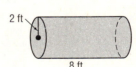

3   **D**

4 What is the surface area of the prism?

   A 120 in²

   B 132 in²

   C 144 in²

   D 288 in²

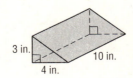

4   **B**

TAKS Practice
Objective 8(8.8)(A) (continued)

Read each question and choose the best answer. Then write the letter for the answer you have chosen in the blank at the right of each question.

5 What is the surface area of the cylinder formed by folding this pattern?

  A 54 m²

  B 36π m²

  C 54π m²

  D 36 + 18π m²

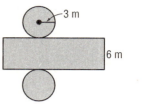

5 ___**C**___

6 What is the surface area of the rectangular prism?

  A 6x unit²

  B 6x^2 unit²

  C 22x^2 unit²

  D 22x^3 unit²

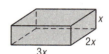

6 ___**C**___

7 A cube has a surface area of 600 square inches. What is the length of an edge of the cube?

  A 100 in.

  B 50 in.

  C 20 in.

  D 10 in.

7 ___**D**___

8 What is the surface area of the rectangular prism formed by folding the pattern?

  A 136 ft²

  B 68 ft²

  C 32 ft²

  D 24 ft²

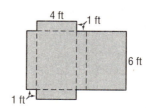

8 ___**B**___

TAKS Practice
Objective 8(8.8)(B)

The student is expected to connect models to formulas for volume of
prisms, cylinders, pyramids, and cones.

*Read each question and choose the best answer. Then write the
letter for the answer you have chosen in the blank at the right of
each question.*

1 What is the volume of the cone?

   A 60π cm^3

   B 120π cm^3

   C 180π cm^3

   D 360π cm^3

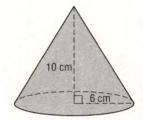

1   **B**

2 What is the volume of the square pyramid?

   A 96 ft^3

   B 48 ft^3

   C 32 ft^3

   D 24 ft^3

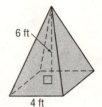

2   **C**

3 What is the volume of this box?

   A 56 m^3

   B 71 m^3

   C 105 m^3

   D 210 m^3

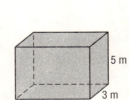

3   **C**

4 The base of a triangular pyramid has an
area of 70 square inches. The height of the
pyramid is 12 inches. What is the volume
of the pyramid?

   A 840 in^3

   B 420 in^3

   C 280 in^3

   D 140 in^3

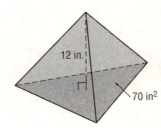

4   **C**

TAKS Practice
Objective 8(8.8)(B) (continued)

Read each question and choose the best answer. Then write the letter for the answer you have chosen in the blank at the right of each question.

5 What is the volume of the cylinder?

   A 48π in^3

   B 96π in^3

   C 144π in^3

   D 192π in^3

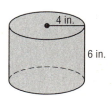

5 _____**B**_____

6 What is the volume of a cube if the length of each edge is 3 units?

Record your answer and fill in the bubbles. Be sure to use the correct place value.

6

7 The volume of a hexagonal prism is 864 cubic centimeters. The height of the prism is 6 centimeters. What is the area of the base of the prism?

   A 432 cm^2

   B 288 cm^2

   C 144 cm^2

   D 48 cm^2

7 _____**C**_____

8 A cylinder has a base whose diameter is 30 feet. The height of the cylinder is 18 feet. What is the volume of the cylinder?

   A 4050π ft^3

   B 1350π ft^3

   C 540π ft^3

   D 180π ft^3

8 _____**A**_____

TAKS Practice
Objective 8(8.8)(C)

The student is expected to estimate answers and use formulas to solve application problems involving surface area and volume.

Read each question and choose the best answer. Then write the letter for the answer you have chosen in the blank at the right of each question.

1 Leonardo is filling a rectangular aquarium for his pet turtles Michaelangelo, Donatello, and Raphael. He pours all of the water from a cylindrical can that is completely full into the aquarium. If the bottom of the aquarium is 12 inches by 18 inches and the can has radius 4 inches and height 9 inches, about how many inches deep will the water be in the aquarium?

A 0.52 in.

B 2.09 in.

C 3.14 in.

D 6.28 in.

1 _____**B**_____

2 Keoka has a circular pool with a radius of 10 feet in her backyard. She wants to put decorative rocks around the outside in a band 2 feet wide and 3 inches deep. About how many cubic feet of rock does she need?

A 415 ft^3

B 113 ft^3

C 46 ft^3

D 35 ft^3

2 _____**D**_____

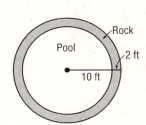

3 What is the approximate volume of the lunch box shown in the diagram? It looks like a rectangular prism with half a circular cylinder for the top.

A 128 in^3

B 134 in^3

C 178 in^3

D 229 in^3

3 _____**C**_____

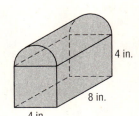

TAKS Practice
Objective 8(8.8)(C) (continued)

Read each question and choose the best answer. Then write the letter for the answer you have chosen in the blank at the right of each question.

4 Two cylindrical tanks are each 20 feet tall. The smaller tank has a radius of 10 feet, and the larger tank has a radius of 14 feet. It takes exactly 5 gallons of paint to paint the sides and top of the smaller tank. How many gallons of paint should be purchased to paint the sides and top of the larger tank? No partial gallons may be purchased.

Record your answer and fill in the bubbles. Be sure to use the correct place value.

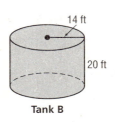

Tank A   Tank B

4

5 A silo has the dimensions shown at the right. If it takes two painters 8 minutes to spray paint 400 square feet, about how long will it take them to paint the sides and top of the silo?

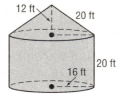

A 60 min
B 70 min
C 80 min
D 90 min

5 ___A___

6 What is the approximate volume of this cold capsule?

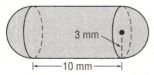

A 509 mm³
B 416 mm³
C 412 mm³
D 396 mm³

6 ___D___

TAKS Practice
Objective 8(8.9)(A)

The student is expected to use the Pythagorean Theorem to solve real-life problems.

Read each question and choose the best answer. Then write the letter for the answer you have chosen in the blank at the right of each question.

1 Penny had to build a ramp over a creek as shown in the diagram. If the sidewalk before the creek is 6 feet above the ground and the creek is 8 feet wide, how long will the ramp be?

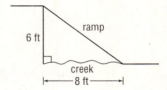

A 2 ft
B 10 ft
C 12 ft
D 14 ft

1 ___**B**___

2 Lance needs to make a right angle for the corner of a foundation. He forms a triangle in the corner. His triangle is 3 feet on one side and 4 feet on another side. How long should the longest side be so he can be sure he has formed a right triangle?

A 1 ft
B 3 ft
C 5 ft
D 7 ft

2 ___**C**___

3 About how much less would you walk if you take the diagonal path from from point A to point B instead of a path around the outside?

A 161 ft
B 242 ft
C 490 ft
D 670 ft

3 ___**A**___

4 Babe needs to pack a golf club in this box. Approximately what is the longest club she can fit in the box?

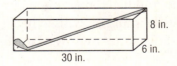

A 27 in.
B 29 in.
C 31 in.
D 33 in.

4 ___**C**___

TAKS Practice
Objective 8(8.9)(A) (continued)

Read each question and choose the best answer. Then write the letter for the answer you have chosen in the blank at the right of each question.

5 Sarah is carrying a piece of wall paneling that is 80 inches wide and 120 inches long into her house. The doorway is 3 feet by 6 feet. Will the panel fit diagonally through the door?

A yes, easily
B yes, barely
C no
D there is not enough information to determine

5 ___**B**___

6 Montrell is planting a row of pecan trees diagonally across a rectangular field that is 500 feet by 1000 feet. The first tree will be planted at a corner of the field. If the trees are 12 feet apart, how many trees will he plant?

A 1118
B 125
C 93
D 90

6 ___**C**___

7 Rocket catches the football at one end of the field. He then runs diagonally the length of the field to score a touchdown. If the field is 100 yards long and 53 yards wide, how many yards does he run? Round your answer to two decimal places.

Record your answer and fill in the bubbles. Be sure to use the correct place value.

7

113.18

8 Martin is putting shingles on his roof. If the span of the roof is 50 feet and it is 7 feet high in the middle, about how many 4-inch-wide rows of shingles will he need for each side if he lets the rows overlap slightly?

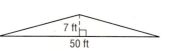

A 160
B 85
C 70
D 65

8 ___**B**___

TAKS Practice
Objective 8(8.9)(B)

The student is expected to use proportional relationships in similar shapes to find missing measurements.

Read each question and choose the best answer. Then write the letter for the answer you have chosen in the blank at the right of each question.

1 Dixie, who is 5 feet tall, is standing near the Tower of Americas, which is 750 feet tall. If Dixie's shadow is 16 feet long, how long is the shadow of the Tower?

  A 2400 ft

  B 600 ft

  C 240 ft

  D 150 ft

1 _____**A**_____

2 Nenna is sailing a boat on Corpus Christi Bay. The boat has two triangular sails that are similar in shape. If the height of the smaller sail is 12 feet and the width 8 feet, what is the width of the larger sail if its height is 20 feet?

  A 10 ft

  B $13\frac{1}{3}$ ft

  C $18\frac{2}{3}$ ft

  D 30 ft

2 _____**B**_____

3 Walt is cross-stitching an owl design on 11-count aida fabric. That means there are 11 stitches per inch on the material. If the finished design will be 8 inches by 10 inches, how many stitches must he do to complete the design?

  A 80

  B 198

  C 8800

  D 9680

3 _____**D**_____

4 The Houston Astrodome has a span of 642 feet and a maximum height of 218 feet. Carlos bought a model of the Astrodome. His model has a span of 15 inches. How many inches is the maximum height of his model? Round your answer to two decimal places.

Record your answer and fill in the bubbles. Be sure to use the correct place value.

4

				5	.	0	9
⓪	⓪	⓪	⓪	●		⓪	⓪
①	①	①	①	①		①	①
②	②	②	②	②		②	②
③	③	③	③	③		③	③
④	④	④	④	④		④	④
⑤	⑤	⑤	⑤	●		⑤	⑤
⑥	⑥	⑥	⑥	⑥		⑥	⑥
⑦	⑦	⑦	⑦	⑦		⑦	⑦
⑧	⑧	⑧	⑧	⑧		⑧	⑧
⑨	⑨	⑨	⑨	⑨		⑨	●

TAKS Practice
Objective 8(8.9)(B) (continued)

Read each question and choose the best answer. Then write the letter for the answer you have chosen in the blank at the right of each question.

5 A sports collectibles store sells two different models of the Sun Bowl. The larger size is 20 inches long and sells for $109. The smaller one is 8 inches long. If the price of the model is directly proportional to its length, what should you expect to pay for the smaller model?

A $272.50
B $172.50
C $43.60
D $13.63

5 ____**C**____

6 Merin has a picture of Roger Staubach that she wants to enlarge. The picture is 4 inches wide and 6 inches long. She wants the width of the enlargement to be 20 inches. What will the length of the enlargement be?

A 10 in.
B $13\frac{2}{3}$ in.
C 18 in.
D 30 in.

6 ____**D**____

7 Teddy's ride-on car is 28 inches long. If it is a scale model of a real car and the scale is 1:7, how many feet long is the real car?

A 4 ft
B $16\frac{1}{3}$ ft
C $19\frac{3}{5}$ ft
D 196 ft

7 ____**B**____

8 Brittany has a toy town. The stop signs in her town are regular octagons with side $\frac{1}{2}$ inch as shown in the diagram. If the side of an actual stop sign is $12\frac{1}{2}$ inches, what is the ratio of similarity between the toy town sign and the actual sign?

$\frac{1}{2}$ in.

A 25:1
B 6:1
C 1:25
D 1:6

8 ____**C**____

TAKS Practice
Objective 8(8.10)(A)

The student is expected to describe the resulting effects on perimeter and area when dimensions of a shape are changed proportionally.

Read each question and choose the best answer. Then write the letter for the answer you have chosen in the blank at the right of each question.

1 When the length of each side of a square is doubled, how does the perimeter change?

   A It stays the same.

   B It is divided in half.

   C It is doubled.

   D It is four times larger.

1 ___**C**___

2 When the length of each side of an equilateral triangle is doubled, how does the area change?

   A It stays the same.

   B It is doubled.

   C It is tripled.

   D It is multiplied by 4.

2 ___**D**___

3 Two rectangles are similar. Their lengths are 6 inches and 10 inches. The area of the smaller rectangle is 24 square inches. What is the area of the larger rectangle to the nearest tenth of a square inch?

   A 66.7 in^2

   B 40 in^2

   C 14.4 in^2

   D 8.6 in^2

3 ___**A**___

4 Two circles have areas 8π square units and 18π square units. If the radius of the smaller circle is a units, what is the radius of the larger circle?

   A $\frac{2a}{3}$ units   **B** $\frac{3a}{2}$ units

   C $\frac{4a}{9}$ units   **D** $\frac{9a}{4}$ units

4 ___**B**___

5 The ratio of the areas of two similar rectangles is 100:49. What is the ratio of the lengths of the rectangles?

   A 10:7

   B 7:10

   C 100:49

   D 49:100

5 ___**A**___

TAKS Practice

Objective 8(8.10)(A) (continued)

Read each question and choose the best answer. Then write the letter for the answer you have chosen in the blank at the right of each question.

6 The rectangles shown in the diagram are similar. The perimeter of *ABCD* is 40 centimeters. What is the perimeter of *WXYZ*?

6

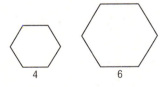

Record your answer and fill in the bubbles. Be sure to use the correct place value.

7 If the two hexagons shown are similar and the area of the smaller is $24\sqrt{3}$, what is the area of the larger hexagon?

7 ___**A**___

A $54\sqrt{3}$

B $36\sqrt{3}$

C $16\sqrt{3}$

D $10\frac{2}{3}\sqrt{3}$

8 If the radius of circle A is 10 times the radius of circle B, which of the following is true?

8 ___**D**___

A The circumference of circle A is 100 times the circumference of circle B.

B The circumference of circle A is 20 times the circumference of circle B.

C The circumference of circle B is 10 times the circumference of circle A.

D The circumference of circle A is 10 times the circumference of circle B.

TAKS Practice
Objective 8(8.10)(B)

The student is expected to describe the resulting effect on volume when dimensions of a solid are changed proportionally.

Read each question and choose the best answer. Then write the letter for the answer you have chosen in the blank at the right of each question.

1 On a rafting trip down the Rio Grande, Nelson lost a rectangular lunch box that was 4 inches by 8 inches by 6 inches. He bought a new rectangular lunch box with dimensions 4 inches by 8 inches by 12 inches. How many times as great is the volume of the new lunch box as the one he lost?

A 8
B 6
C 4
D 2

1 _____ **D** _____

2 Mimi has two jewelry boxes that are similar cylinders. If the ratio of the radii is 5:7, what is the ratio of the volume of the smaller cylinder to that of the larger cylinder?

A 125:343
B 25:49
C 343:125
D 49:25

2 _____ **A** _____

3 The ratio of the volumes of two spheres is 125:8. What is the ratio of their radii?

A 125:8
B 5:2
C 2:5
D 25:4

3 _____ **B** _____

4 The surface areas of one face of two cubes are 49 square centimeters and 100 square centimeters. What is the ratio of the volume of the smaller box to that of the larger box?

A 7:10   **B** 49:100
C 343:1000   **D** 2401:10,000

4 _____ **C** _____

5 The ratio of the radii of two spheres is 3:5. What is the ratio of their volumes?

A 3:5   **B** 9:25
C 9:15   **D** 27:125

5 _____ **D** _____

TAKS Practice
Objective 8(8.10)(B) (continued)

Read each question and choose the best answer. Then write the letter for the answer you have chosen in the blank at the right of each question.

6 The edges of cube A are half as long as the edges of cube B. The edges of cube C are twice as long as the edges of cube B. What is the ratio of the volume of cube A to the volume of cube C?

6 _____ **D**_____

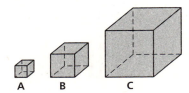

A 4:1
B 1:8
C 1:16
D 1:64

7 Boxes A and B are rectangular boxes. The bottom of box B is half as long and half as wide as the bottom of box A. The heights of the boxes are equal. What is the ratio of the volume of box A to the volume of box B?

7 _____ **B**_____

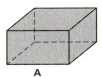

A 8:1
B 4:1
C 2:1
D 1:2

8 A cylindrical tank will hold 1000 gallons of water. Another tank has a radius and height that are 1.6 times those of the first tank. How many gallons will the larger tank hold?

Record your answer and fill in the bubbles. Be sure to use the correct place value.

8

4	0	9	6	.			
⓪	●	⓪	⓪		⓪	⓪	⓪
①	①	①	①		①	①	①
②	②	②	②		②	②	②
③	③	③	③		③	③	③
●	④	④	④		④	④	④
⑤	⑤	⑤	⑤		⑤	⑤	⑤
⑥	⑥	⑥	●		⑥	⑥	⑥
⑦	⑦	⑦	⑦		⑦	⑦	⑦
⑧	⑧	⑧	⑧		⑧	⑧	⑧
⑨	⑨	●	⑨		⑨	⑨	⑨

TAKS Practice
Objective 9(8.1)(B)

The student is expected to select and use appropriate forms of rational numbers to solve real-life problems including those involving proportional relationships.

Read each question and choose the best answer. Then write the letter for the answer you have chosen in the blank at the right of each question.

1 The value of the stock of a computer company rose from $17.50 to $18.25 per share. By how much did the value of 100 shares of the stock increase?

   A $1825.00   **B** $1737.50

   C $100.00   **D** $75.00

1 ____**D**____

2 Big T store sells peanut butter in three different sized jars.

   8 ounces for $1.79
   16 ounces for $3.39
   30 ounces for $6.79

   Which container is the best buy?

   A the 8-ounce jar   **B** the 16-ounce jar

   C the 30-ounce jar   **D** They are all equally good buys.

2 ____**B**____

3 Reggie gets to work at 8:15 A.M. and leaves at 5:30 P.M. He takes from 12:30 P.M. until 1:00 P.M. for lunch. How many hours does he work in one day?

   Record your answer and fill in the bubbles. Be sure to use the correct place value.

3

				.			
			8	.	7	5	
⓪	⓪	⓪	⓪		⓪	⓪	⓪
①	①	①	①		①	①	①
②	②	②	②		②	②	②
③	③	③	③		③	③	③
④	④	④	④		④	④	④
⑤	⑤	⑤	⑤		⑤	●	⑤
⑥	⑥	⑥	⑥		⑥	⑥	⑥
⑦	⑦	⑦	⑦		●	⑦	⑦
⑧	⑧	⑧	●		⑧	⑧	⑧
⑨	⑨	⑨	⑨		⑨	⑨	⑨

4 Leona worked for 37.5 hours last week. Her pay for the week, before taxes were deducted, was $346.88. How much did she earn per hour?

   A $9.50   **B** $9.25

   C $9.00   **D** $8.67

4 ____**B**____

5 Kostadinova jumped 2.09 meters in the high jump in 1987. In 1996 Austin jumped 2.39 meters. Sotomajor set the high jump record in 1993 with a jump of 2.45 meters. How many meters higher was Sotomajor's jump than Kostadinova's?

   A 0.36 m   **B** 0.30 m

   C 0.26 m   **D** 0.06 m

5 ____**A**____

TAKS Practice
Objective 9(8.3)(B)

The student is expected to estimate and find solutions to application problems involving percents and proportional relationships such as similarity and rates.

Read each question and choose the best answer. Then write the letter for the answer you have chosen in the blank at the right of each question.

1 It was estimated that 471 sea turtle eggs hatched on South Padre Island in the summer of 2002. If 13% of the turtles survived, about how many survived?

Record your answer and fill in the bubbles. Be sure to use the correct place value.

1

			6	1	.			
⓪	⓪	⓪	⓪		⓪	⓪	⓪
①	①	①	●		①	①	①
②	②	②	②		②	②	②
③	③	③	③		③	③	③
④	④	④	④		④	④	④
⑤	⑤	⑤	⑤		⑤	⑤	⑤
⑥	⑥	●	⑥		⑥	⑥	⑥
⑦	⑦	⑦	⑦		⑦	⑦	⑦
⑧	⑧	⑧	⑧		⑧	⑧	⑧
⑨	⑨	⑨	⑨		⑨	⑨	⑨

2 The Panhandle Café publishes discount coupons in the local newspaper. If Tim has a 10% discount coupon and his meal costs $5.99, how much will he have to pay before tax?

A $6.59
B $5.93
C $5.39
D $0.60

2 ___**C**___

3 Texas Stadium has 63,855 seats. If it is 85% filled, about how many people are in the stadium?

A 60,000
B 55,000
C 50,000
D 45,000

3 ___**B**___

4 There is a scale model of LBJ's oval office at the LBJ Library and Museum in Austin. The scale for the model is 7:8. If the distance from the desk to a door in the scale model is x feet, what expression represents the distance in the actual office?

A $\frac{7}{8}x$ ft
B $\frac{8}{7}x$ ft
C $x + \frac{7}{8}$ ft
D $x + \frac{7}{8}x$ ft

4 ___**B**___

5 The area of the Toledo Bend Reserve is 182,000 acres. The area of Sam Houston National Forest is 161,841 acres. The area of Sam Houston Forest is about what percent of the area of Toledo Bend Reserve?

A 60%
B 70%
C 90%
D 80%

5 ___**C**___

TAKS Practice
Objective 9(8.3)(B) (continued)

*Read each question and choose the best answer. Then write the
letter for the answer you have chosen in the blank at the right of
each question.*

6 Ruth is walking on the beach at Galveston. She sees 27 red umbrellas,
12 blue umbrellas, and 15 yellow umbrellas. What percent of the
umbrellas that she sees are red?

  A 27%

  B 42%

  C 50%

  D 60%

6 ____**C**____

7 Bryce has a batting average of .278. If he comes to bat 80 times in the
month of August, about how many hits will he get?

  A 22

  B 27

  C 28

  D 30

7 ____**A**____

8 A mousepad is regularly priced at $15.99. If it is on sale for $12.79,
about what is the percent of discount?

  A 80%

  B 25%

  C 23%

  D 20%

8 ____**D**____

9 Arnie earns 3% interest on his 12-month certificate of deposit. If he
invests $12,000, how much interest will his certificate earn for the year?

Record your answer and fill in the bubbles. Be sure to use the correct
place value.

9

3	6	0	.			
⓪	⓪	⓪	●	⓪	⓪	⓪
①	①	①	①	①	①	①
②	②	②	②	②	②	②
③	●	③	③	③	③	③
④	④	④	④	④	④	④
⑤	⑤	⑤	⑤	⑤	⑤	⑤
⑥	⑥	●	⑥	⑥	⑥	⑥
⑦	⑦	⑦	⑦	⑦	⑦	⑦
⑧	⑧	⑧	⑧	⑧	⑧	⑧
⑨	⑨	⑨	⑨	⑨	⑨	⑨

10 What is the amount of sales tax at 6.25% owed on a DVD that costs
$23.99?

  A $1.50

  B $1.40

  C $14.99

  D $25.49

10 ____**A**____

TAKS Practice
Objective 9(8.11)(A)

The student is expected to find the probabilities of compound events.

Read each question and choose the best answer. Then write the letter for the answer you have chosen in the blank at the right of each question.

1 A couple is planning to have 3 children. What is the probability that the first two are girls and the third is a boy?

   A $\frac{1}{8}$ **B** $\frac{3}{8}$

   C $\frac{1}{2}$ **D** $\frac{2}{3}$

1   **A**

2 Two cards are selected from an ordinary deck of 52 cards. What is the probability that both are hearts?

   A $\frac{2}{13}$ **B** $\frac{1}{16}$

   C $\frac{1}{17}$ **D** $\frac{1}{156}$

2   **C**

3 Venice tosses two dice. What is the probability that he tosses a sum of 8?

   A $\frac{5}{12}$ **B** $\frac{1}{3}$

   C $\frac{1}{6}$ **D** $\frac{5}{36}$

3   **D**

4 Francisco has 10 marbles in a bag. Three of the marbles are red, 4 are blue, 2 are black, and 1 is yellow. If he picks 2 marbles from the bag, what is the probability that he draws a red marble first and then a yellow marble? He does not replace the first marble after he takes it out.

   A $\frac{3}{100}$ **B** $\frac{1}{30}$

   C $\frac{1}{3}$ **D** $\frac{37}{90}$

4   **B**

5 Sixteen students were polled about their favorite type of music. Eight liked only alternative, 6 liked only rock, and 2 liked both alternative and rock. If a student is selected at random from this group, what is the probability that he or she likes rock music? Write your answer as a decimal.

Record your answer and fill in the bubbles. Be sure to use the correct place value.

5

			0	.	5		
⓪	⓪	⓪	●		⓪	⓪	⓪
①	①	①	①		①	①	①
②	②	②	②		②	②	②
③	③	③	③		③	③	③
④	④	④	④		④	④	④
⑤	⑤	⑤	⑤		●	⑤	⑤
⑥	⑥	⑥	⑥		⑥	⑥	⑥
⑦	⑦	⑦	⑦		⑦	⑦	⑦
⑧	⑧	⑧	⑧		⑧	⑧	⑧
⑨	⑨	⑨	⑨		⑨	⑨	⑨

TAKS Practice
Objective 9(8.11)(B)

The student is expected to use theoretical probabilities and experimental results to make predictions and decisions.

Read each question and choose the best answer. Then write the letter for the answer you have chosen in the blank at the right of each question.

1 Dion flipped two fair coins 20 times. The results are shown in this table. Based on these experimental results, what is the probability of flipping two heads?

Result	Number of Times
2 heads	6
1 head, 1 tail	11
2 tails	3

A $\frac{1}{2}$

B $\frac{3}{7}$

C $\frac{3}{10}$

D $\frac{1}{4}$

1 ___**C**___

2 If Jocelyn tosses a fair die 36 times, how many times would she expect it to show a number greater than 4?

Record your answer and fill in the bubbles. Be sure to use the correct place value.

2

3 In one city in Texas, there are 105 boys born for every 100 girls. If 656 babies were born at a hospital in the city this year, how many would you expect to be boys?

A 336

B 328

C 320

D 210

3 ___**A**___

4 Workers in a factory that makes flashlights know that 3 out of every 100 are defective. What is the probability that a flashlight chosen at random is defective?

A $\frac{1}{50}$

B $\frac{3}{100}$

C $\frac{3}{97}$

D $\frac{97}{100}$

4 ___**B**___

TAKS Practice
Objective 9(8.11)(B) (continued)

Read each question and choose the best answer. Then write the letter for the answer you have chosen in the blank at the right of each question.

5 This table gives the ages and genders of people at a sports memorabilia show. What is the probability that a person chosen at random at the show is between the ages of 19 and 35 and is female?

Ages	Male	Female
0–18	42	20
19–35	66	54
35–60	28	34
over 60	12	16

A $\frac{95}{136}$

B $\frac{68}{136}$

C $\frac{33}{136}$

D $\frac{27}{136}$

5 ____**D**____

6 A used car lot owner says there is a 30% probability that a person who wants to buy a car will ask for a red car. How many of the next 200 people who come to the lot would you expect to ask for a red car?

A 60

B 50

C 40

D 30

6 ____**A**____

7 This table shows information on savings accounts offered by several banks in Texas. If one of these banks is chosen at random, what is the probability that its savings rate is 2%?

Interest Rate	Number of Banks
1.0%	7
1.25%	9
1.5%	15
2.0%	19

A 9%

B 20%

C 25%

D 38%

7 ____**D**____

8 A company that makes widgets claims there is only a 0.008 probability that a customer who orders a widget will receive one that is defective. On the basis of this information, how many of the next 7000 widgets shipped would you expect to be free of defects?

A 9920

B 6944

C 992

D 560

8 ____**B**____

TAKS Practice
Objective 9(8.12)(A)

The student is expected to select the appropriate measure of central tendency to describe a set of data for a particular purpose.

Read each question and choose the best answer. Then write the letter for the answer you have chosen in the blank at the right of each question.

1 The scores on the most recent test in Mr. Lucas's science class are shown below. Is the mean, the median, or the mode the best measure of how a typical student performed on the test?

100, 100, 100, 98, 97, 86, 85, 85, 84, 84,
82, 78, 78, 76, 70, 69, 67, 60, 60, 55

A mean
B median
C mode
D All are equally good.

1 _____**B**_____

2 This chart shows data about different kinds of livestock animals in Texas in January 1999.

Livestock	Number (millions)
cattle	1.4
sheep	1.4
hogs	0.64
chickens	24.4

What is the mean number (in millions) of livestock animals in these categories?

Record your answer and fill in the bubbles. Be sure to use the correct place value.

2

			6	.	9	6
⓪	⓪	⓪	⓪	⓪	⓪	⓪
①	①	①	①	①	①	①
②	②	②	②	②	②	②
③	③	③	③	③	③	③
④	④	④	④	④	④	④
⑤	⑤	⑤	⑤	⑤	⑤	⑤
⑥	⑥	⑥	●	⑥	●	⑥
⑦	⑦	⑦	⑦	⑦	⑦	⑦
⑧	⑧	⑧	⑧	⑧	⑧	⑧
⑨	⑨	⑨	⑨	●	⑨	⑨

TAKS Practice
Objective 9(8.12)(A) (continued)

Read each question and choose the best answer. Then write the letter for the answer you have chosen in the blank at the right of each question.

3 This chart gives the monthly average temperature in Houston.

Month	Jan	Feb	Mar	Apr	May	Jun	Jul	Aug	Sep	Oct	Nov	Dec
Temp. (°F)	50	54	62	68	75	80	83	82	78	70	60	54

Which of the following statements is correct?

A The median is 81.5, and the mode is 54.

B The median is 81.5, and the mode is 33.

C The median is 69, and the mode is 68.

D The median is 69, and the mode is 54.

3 ___**D**___

4 This chart shows the mean SAT mathematics scores for several states in 1999. What is the range of these scores?

State	Score
Minnesota	598
Illinois	585
Texas	499
Virginia	499
South Dakota	475

A 123

B 531.2

C 499

D 536.5

4 ___**A**___

5 This table gives the enrollment in several Texas universities in 1999.

School	Enrollment
University of Texas, Austin	48,906
Texas Christian University	7395
Southern Methodist University	10,038
Baylor University	12,967
Texas A & M University	43,389

At what school does the median enrollment occur?

A Southern Methodist University

B University of Texas, Austin

C Baylor University

D Texas Christian University

5 ___**C**___

Name _____   Date _____

TAKS Practice
Objective 9(8.12)(C)

The student is expected to construct circle graphs, bar graphs, and histograms, with and without technology.

Read each question and choose the best answer. Then write the letter for the answer you have chosen in the blank at the right of each question.

1 The bar graph shows the number of West Nile virus cases in August 2002. About how many more cases did Mississippi have than Texas?

    A 48

    B 40

    C 15

    D 35

West Nile Virus Cases in August 2002

1   **D**

2 This circle graph shows the top shopping Web sites as of August 1999. If there were a total of 43,904 hits on these 5 sites together, about how many hits were there on Amazon.com? Round to the nearest hundred.

    A 9500

    B 11,000

    C 11,700

    D 11,600

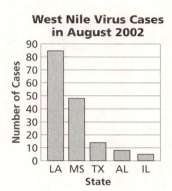

Top Shopping Web Sites (as of August 1999)

2   **D**

3 To construct a circle graph showing the length of time each of the plays listed in this table were on Broadway, about how many whole degrees would you use to represent *Les Miserables*?

Show	Number of Performances
Cats	6949
Les Miserables	5031
Grease	3388
Fiddler on the Roof	3242

Record your answer and fill in the bubbles. Be sure to use the correct place value.

3

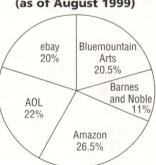

TAKS Practice

Objective 9(8.12)(C) (continued)

Read each question and choose the best answer. Then write the letter for the answer you have chosen in the blank at the right of each question.

4 This table gives the number of Super Bowl appearances by several NFL teams. Cookie is making a bar graph to illustrate the data. Which of the following would be a reasonable scale for her to use on the vertical (number of wins) axis?

4 __**B**__

Team	Number of Super Bowl Appearances
Dallas Cowboys	5
San Francisco 49ers	5
Pittsburgh Steelers	4
Green Bay Packers	3
Denver Broncos	2

A 0 to 20, with intervals of 1
B 0 to 5, with intervals of 1
C 0 to 100, with intervals of 10
D 0 to 10, with intervals of 10

5 This stacked bar graph shows the number of wins and losses for the Texas NBA basketball teams during the shortened 1998-1999 season. How many more games did the Spurs win than the Rockets?

5 __**A**__

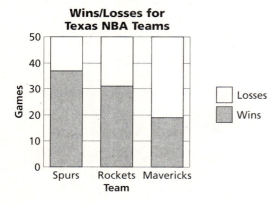

A 6
B 31
C 47
D 50

Name _____ Date _____

TAKS Practice
Objective 9(8.13)(B)

The student is expected to recognize misuses of graphical or numerical information and evaluate predictions and conclusions based on data analysis.

Read each question and choose the best answer. Then write the letter for the answer you have chosen in the blank at the right of each question.

1 The temperatures in Bracketville on three consecutive days in July are shown in this bar graph. Andy concluded that it was much cooler on July 2 and 3 than it was on July 1. What probably caused his incorrect conclusion?

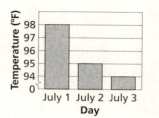

A decreased humidity
B not enough bars on the bar graph
C a misleading vertical scale on the bar graph
D inaccurate temperature readings

1 __**C**__

2 The Midwestern Credit Union surveyed fifty members about their interest in retirement savings accounts. The results of the survey are shown in the table. Which of the following reasons could cause this data to be an inaccurate representation of the opinions of all the credit union members?

Opinion	Number of People
interested	3
not interested	47

A Everyone was surveyed between the hours of 9 A.M. and 4 P.M.
B Everyone surveyed had a checking account.
C Everyone surveyed had an office job.
D Everyone surveyed was under the age of 21.

2 __**D**__

3 The circle graph is intended to show what percent of students at a certain college watch the given television shows. From this graph it may appear that *Law and Order* is the most watched of the four shows. Is this a correct conclusion and why?

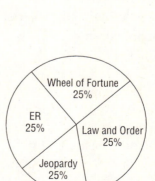

A Yes, since it appears to be represented by the largest section.
B No, since the percents do not match the sizes of the sections.
C No, *Jeopardy* is the most watched show.
D No, since college students may not own TV sets.

3 __**B**__

TAKS Test Prep, Grade 9   **79**

TAKS Practice

Objective 9(8.13)(B) (continued)

Read each question and choose the best answer. Then write the letter for the answer you have chosen in the blank at the right of each question.

4 The Moores have two children, both girls. Which of the following is a correct conclusion about their next child?

    A There is a $\frac{2}{3}$ probability that the child will be a girl.

    B There is a $\frac{2}{3}$ probability that the child will be a boy.

    C There is a $\frac{1}{2}$ probability that the child will be a boy.

    D There is a probability of 1 that the child will be a girl.

4   **C**

5 Sammy is batting .318, while Mark is batting .326. What information does this give you?

    A the percentage of times at bat that they got base hits

    B the number of hits that were not base hits

    C the number of times each of them batted

    D the number of hits each of them got

5   **A**

6 A pet store conducted a survey to see what pets were already owned by the people who came into the store. They put colored cards by the door and asked people to drop a card into the survey box to tell what kind of pet they owned: yellow for fish, blue for a dog, red for a cat, and green for a bird. What conclusion can they draw when they count the cards of each color at the end of the day?

    A how many people were in the store that day

    B how many people own only one pet

    C how many people do not yet own a pet

    D No useful conclusion is possible.

6   **D**

7 A small company has only ten employees. The president is the highest-paid person and earns $120,000 per year. The range of the salaries is $90,000. What is one reason that this information does not give an adequate idea of what the people in the company earn?

    A You know nothing about how much profit the company makes.

    B You can say only what the maximum and minimum salaries are.

    C You do not know how many people the company plans to hire.

    D You do not know how long each employee has worked at the company.

7   **B**

Name _____ Date _____

TAKS Practice
Objective 10(8.14)(A) ——————————————

The student is expected to identify and apply mathematics to everyday experiences, to activities in and outside of school, with other disciplines, and with other mathematical topics.

Read each question and choose the best answer. Then write the letter for the answer you have chosen in the blank at the right of each question.

1 Reba earned $38,500 during 2001. According to the income tax table below, how much tax must she pay?

1 _____ **A** _____

If income is over	but not over	enter	of the amount over
$0	$27,050	15%	$0
$27,050	$65,550	$4057.50 + 27.5%	$27,050
$65,550	$136,750	$14,645.00 + 30.5%	$65,550
$136,750	$297,350	$36,361.00 + 35.5%	$136,750
$297,350	—	$93,374.00 + 39.1%	$297,350

A $7206.25

B $5775.00

C $4085.00

D $4000.85

2 Fred has a checking account. His balance on August 1 was $52.76. During August he deposited one paycheck for $677.51 and wrote the following checks. What was the balance in his account at the end of August (assuming that all of the checks he wrote cleared)?

2

Check	Amount
discount store	$49.20
grocery store	$72.40
cash	$100.00
electric bill	$26.89
rent	$356.00
cell phone bill	$19.99

Record your answer and fill in the bubbles. Be sure to use the correct place value.

Name _____   Date _____

TAKS Practice
Objective 10(8.14)(A) (continued) ━━━━━━━

Read each question and choose the best answer. Then write the letter for the answer you have chosen in the balnk at the right of each question.

3 Alexei bought 6 pens for $0.99 each and 2 pads of paper for $0.48 each. He gave the clerk at the Laredo high school bookstore a $20 bill. If the tax was 6.25%, how much change did he receive?

   A $6.90

   B $7.33

   C $11.67

   D $12.67

3 ____**D**____

4 Chester has a rectangular corral that is 300 feet long and 100 feet wide. He needs to buy fence to enclose it. If an 8-foot section of fence costs $29.95, how many 8-foot sections does he need to buy?

   A 50

   B 100

   C 800

   D 3750

4 ____**B**____

5 What is the area of the trapezoidal lot shown in the diagram?

   A 900,000 ft^2

   B 450,000 ft^2

   C 12,000 ft^2

   D 9000 ft^2

5 ____**C**____

6 Nell is putting quarry tile in her kitchen. The kitchen is 12 feet by 18 feet. If the tiles are squares 18 inches on each side, how many tiles does she need?

   A 1728

   B 216

   C 144

   D 96

6 ____**D**____

82 *TAKS Test Prep, Grade 9*

TAKS Practice
Objective 10(8.14)(B)

The student is expected to use a problem-solving model that incorporates understanding the problem, making a plan, carrying out the plan, and evaluating the solution for reasonableness.

Read each question and choose the best answer. Then write the letter for the answer you have chosen in the blank at the right of each question.

1 José is a student at State College. He uses his debit card to buy 3 CDs for a total of $31.95. Before his purchase he had $129 in his checking account. What should he do to calculate his new balance?

  A Subtract 129 from 31.95.
  B Subtract 31.95 from 129.
  C Add 31.95 to 129.
  D Multiply 31.95 by 129.

1 ____**B**____

2 Rita counted 6 jet skis and 10 pontoon boats on Lake Texoma. If there was one person on each jet ski and an average of 6 people on the pontoon boats, how many people did she see out on the lake? Which operations can you use to solve this problem?

  A addition and subtraction
  B division and addition
  C multiplication and addition
  D division and subtraction

2 ____**C**____

3 Drew threw a football from a height of 6 feet. The ball traveled 50 yards down the field. If the height h of the ball at time t is given by the equation $h = -16t^2 + 20t + 6$, what is the maximum height reached by the football? What would you do to solve this problem?

  A Substitute 6 into the equation for h and solve for t.
  B Substitute 50 into the equation for t and solve for h.
  C Graph the function, trace the graph, and find the x-coordinate of the vertex.
  D Graph the function, trace the graph, and find the y-coordinate of the vertex.

3 ____**D**____

4 Pat used indirect measurement to calculate the height of the Capital Building. Which of the following answers would be reasonable?

  A 2000 ft
  B 200 ft
  C 20 ft
  D 2 ft

4 ____**B**____

TAKS Practice
Objective 10(8.14)(C)

The student is expected to select or develop an appropriate problem-solving strategy from a variety of different types, including drawing a picture, looking for a pattern, systematic guessing and checking, acting it out, making a table, working a simpler problem, or working backwards to solve a problem.

Read each question and choose the best answer. Then write the letter for the answer you have chosen in the blank at the right of each question.

1 Alice and Jane are going to meet for coffee at the donut shop before school. They live 0.5 miles apart. The donut shop is 0.3 miles from each of their houses. Which of the following diagrams could be used to find the location of the donut shop?

1 _____ **C**

A

B
●————●————●
Alice   Jane   Donut
                 Shop

C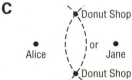

D
          ● Donut
          ┊ Shop
●- - - - -┘
Alice Jane

2 The product of two consecutive integers is 8742. How could you find the numbers?

2 _____ **A**

A Guess one of the numbers, add 1, and multiply. Then adjust the guess and continue until the correct numbers are found.

B Divide 8742 by 2 to get one of the numbers. Then add 1 to get the other number.

C Find the square root of 8742 to get one of the numbers. Then add 1 to get the other number.

D Find the square root of 8742 to get one of the numbers. Then divide 8742 by the result to get the other number.

3 Ben is three years older than Shumaki. The sum of their ages is 53. How could you find how old Shumaki is?

3 _____ **C**

A Subtract 3 from 50 to get Shumaki's age.

B First divide 53 by 2 to get Ben's age.

C List pairs of numbers that are 3 apart and their sums. Keep going until you get to a sum of 53.

D List multiples of 3. Keep going until you get to 53.

TAKS Practice
Objective 10(8.15)(A)

The student is expected to communicate mathematical ideas using language, efficient tools, appropriate units, and graphical, numerical, physical, or algebraic mathematical models.

Read each question and choose the best answer. Then write the letter for the answer you have chosen in the blank at the right of each question.

1 Which of the following would be a good way to show the range and median of the quiz scores given in the stem-and-leaf plot?

Stem	Leaf
1	2
2	0 7 8
3	2 5 6 6 8
4	1 2 3 3 6 9

1|2 = 12

A Draw a circle graph.
B Draw a bar graph.
C Write an equation.
D Draw a box-and-whisker plot.

1 ____**D**____

2 The captain of a plane is going to make an announcement to the passengers to let them know the speed of the plane. Which would be an appropriate unit of speed for him to use?

A centimeters per second
B centimeters per hour
C miles per hour
D miles per second

2 ____**C**____

3 Which of the following would be the most appropriate unit for the volume of a shoe box?

A cubic inches
B cubic yards
C grams
D kilograms

3 ____**A**____

4 Claudio wants to give a class report on how the daily high temperature in San Antonio has changed over a two-week period. Which would be an appropriate way for him to present his data?

A box-and-whisker plot
B line graph
C circle graph
D frequency table

4 ____**B**____

TAKS Practice
Objective 10(8.15)(A) (continued)

Read each question and choose the best answer. Then write the letter for the answer you have chosen in the blank at the right of each question.

5 Angel is trying to find the height of a building. Which of the following would be a reasonable method for him to use?

  A He could release a balloon at ground level, time it to see how long it takes to reach the top, then multiply by the speed of the balloon.

  B He could throw a rope up to the top, pull it down, and measure the rope.

  C He could use the stairway to go to the top and use a stopwatch to see how long it takes.

  D He could measure his own height, the length of his shadow, and the length of the building's shadow and use a proportion.

5 ____**D**____

6 Which of the following would be a reasonable procedure for Jill to use to estimate the number of fish in Lake Austin?

  A Empty the water out of the lake and count the fish.

  B Catch all the fish in the lake and count them.

  C Catch some fish, tag them, put them back, then later catch more and see what percent of them are tagged.

  D Dip a one-gallon bucket into the lake, pull it up, and count the number of fish. Multiply by the number of gallons of water in the lake.

6 ____**C**____

7 Which of the following equations could Wilhemina use to represent the time t, in hours, it takes to drive 100 miles at a speed of s miles per hour?

  A $t = 100s$

  B $t = \dfrac{100}{s}$

  C $\dfrac{t}{s} = 100$

  D $s = 100t$

7 ____**B**____

8 Which of the following equations could Forest use to represent the cost c of a box of chocolates if the chocolates sell for \$7.99 per pound and the box contains w pounds?

  A $w = \dfrac{7.99}{c}$

  B $w = 7.99c$

  C $c = \dfrac{w}{7.99}$

  D $c = 7.99w$

8 ____**D**____

TAKS Practice
Objective 10(8.16)(A)

The student is expected to make conjectures from patterns or sets of examples and nonexamples.

Read each question and choose the best answer. Then write the letter for the answer you have chosen in the blank at the right of each question.

1 Using the data shown in this table, what would you expect the sum of the measures of the interior angles of an 8-sided polygon to be?

Number of sides	3	4	5	6	7
Sum of measures of interior angles	180°	360°	540°	720°	900°

Record your answer and fill in the bubbles. Be sure to use the correct place value.

1

1	0	8	0	.			

2 Garrison and Latisha are playing a game in which Latisha must deduce what property Garrison is thinking of. If all of the figures in Group A have the property that Garrison is thinking of and those in Group B do not have the property, which of the following figures also has the property?

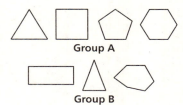

Group A

Group B

A

B

C

D

2 _____ **B**

3 What is a reasonable conjecture for the next number in the pattern?

2, 6, 24, 120, 720, …

A 1020   **B** 5040

C 14,320   **D** 40,320

3 _____ **B**

4 What is a reasonable conjecture for the next number in the pattern?

2, 3, 6, 4, 5, 20, 6, 7, 42, 8, 9, …

A 10

B 56

C 72

D 90

4 _____ **C**

TAKS Practice
Objective 10(8.16)(B)

The student is expected to validate his/her conclusions using mathematical properties and relationships.

Read each question and choose the best answer. Then write the letter for the answer you have chosen in the blank at the right of each question.

1 Terri bet Lisa a candy bar that she, Terri, could throw a football at 40 feet per second from a height of 5 feet and it would reach a height of 41 feet. The height of the football h at time t is given by the equation $h = -16t^2 + 40t + 5$. Who won the candy bar?

    A Terri, because the ball reaches a maximum height of 41 ft.

    B Lisa, because the ball never reaches 41 ft.

    C Terri, because the ball goes much higher than 41 ft.

    D The winner cannot be determined.

1 ____**B**____

2 Rich found $\sqrt{60}$ to be 12.5. Which of the following reasons could Nancy have used to tell him his answer was not possible?

    A 60 divided by 2 is 30.

    B $\sqrt{60} = 2\sqrt{15}$, so $\sqrt{60}$ should be 2(7.5) or 15.

    C $12.5^2 = 156.25$ and $156.25 \neq 60$.

    D $60^2 = 3600$ and 12.5^2 is only 156.25.

2 ____**C**____

3 To convince a friend that $x^2 + 4x + 5$ is positive for all values of x, what would be the most helpful way to rewrite the expression?

    A $x^2 + (4x + 5)$

    B $(x^2 + 2x) + (2x + 5)$

    C $x(x + 4) + 5$

    D $(x + 2)^2 + 1$

3 ____**D**____

4 Marcelina left home and rode her bike 2 miles north, 3 miles east, another 4 miles north, and 5 more miles east. If she turns around and bikes straight home on the diagonal, how many miles will she have to ride to get home?

Record your answer and fill in the bubbles. Be sure to use the correct place value.

4

Name _____   Date _____

TAKS Practice
Sample Test 1 _____

Read each question and choose the best answer. Then write the letter for the answer you have chosen in the blank at the right of each question.

1 Cindy works out lifting weights. Data on the number of reps she has done in the first four weeks is given in the table. If the pattern continues, how many reps will she do during week eight? **1A(b)(1)(E)**

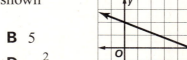

Week	1	2	3	4
Number of Reps	7	12	17	22

   A 42   **B** 40

   C 32   **D** 27

1   **A**

2 What is the *x*-intercept of the graph shown at the right? **3A(c)(2)(E)**

   A 6   **B** 5

   C $\frac{5}{2}$ **D** $-\frac{2}{5}$

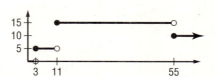

2   **B**

3 Which relationship could be shown by this graph? **2A(b)(2)(C)**

   A height of a tree as a function of its age

   B interest paid on a savings account as a function of time

   C admission price to a water park as a function of age

   D distance traveled for 4 hours as a function of speed

3   **C**

4 Asia buys a hamburger for $1.99, fries for $0.87, and a chocolate milkshake for $2.25 at the corner hamburger stand. What is her total bill before tax? **10(8.14)(A)**

Record your answer and fill in the bubbles. Be sure to use the correct place value.

5 What is the slope of the line shown in the graph at the right? **3A(c)(2)(A)**

   A $-\frac{5}{3}$ **B** $-\frac{3}{5}$

   C $\frac{3}{5}$ **D** $\frac{5}{3}$

5   **D**

Go on

TAKS Practice
Sample Test 1 (continued)

Read each question and choose the best answer. Then write the letter for the answer you have chosen in the blank at the right of each question.

6 Willow was solving $x^2 + 5x = -6$. This is her work. What mistake did she make? **10(8.14)(B)**

6 ____**A**____

$$x^2 + 5x = -6$$
$$x(x + 5) = -6$$
$$x = -6 \text{ or } x + 5 = -6$$
$$= -6 \qquad\qquad = -11$$

A She should have set one side of the equation equal to 0 before factoring.
B She should have used $x = -2$ and $x + 5 = 3$.
C She should have used $x = -6$ and $x + 5 = 1$.
D She should only have 1 answer.

7 The supports for a swing set are in a "V" shape. The supports are 15 feet long and 18 feet apart at the base. How many feet above the ground is the top of the swing set? **8(8.9)(A)**

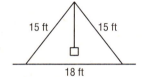

7 ____**C**____

A 9 ft   **B** 10 ft
C 12 ft   **D** 15 ft

8 Lori can stay at the Lights Out Motel for $85 per night, including breakfast, or at the Royal Vista Hotel for x dollars per night. The Royal Vista does not include breakfast. She figures she will spend an average of $38 per day for lunch and dinner together or $48 per day for all three meals. For what values of x would the Royal Vista be less expensive than the Lights Out? **4A(c)(3)(B)**

8 ____**A**____

A $x < 75$ **B** $x > 10$
C $x < 123$ **D** $x > 48$

9 Which is the equation of a line that passes through $(9, 1)$ and is parallel to the line $y = \frac{2}{3}x + 6$? **3A(c)(2)(D)**

9 ____**D**____

A $y = \frac{2}{3}x + 1$ **B** $y = -\frac{3}{2}x + 1$

C $y = -\frac{3}{2}x + \frac{29}{2}$ **D** $y = \frac{2}{3}x - 5$

10 Two octagons are similar. If the ratio of their perimeters is 6:7, what is the ratio of their areas? **8(8.10)(A)**

10 ____**C**____

A 6:7   **B** 12:14
C 36:49   **D** 216:343

Go on

TAKS Practice

Sample Test 1 (continued)

Read each question and choose the best answer. Then write the letter for the answer you have chosen in the blank at the right of each question.

11 Taylor bought a 3-month old steer that weighed 143 pounds. He raised it, groomed it, and sold it at the State Fair in 1999 for $70,000. If the steer tripled its weight every 7 months, how much did it weigh when he sold it at the age of 17 months? **5A(d)(3)(A)**

A 429 lb   **B** 572 lb
C 1287 lb   **D** 2061 lb

11 ____**C**____

12 Which of the following are the factors of $2x^2 - 5x - 12$? **2A(b)(4)(A)**

A $(2x - 4)(x + 3)$ **B** $(2x + 3)(x - 4)$
C $(2x - 3)(x + 4)$ **D** $(2x - 6)(x + 2)$

12 ____**B**____

13 The total cost T of painting Mrs. Murray's office is given by $T = 15h + 12(8)$, where h is the number of hours the painter works, 12 is the price in dollars of a gallon of paint, and 8 is the number of gallons of paint needed. What is the dependent variable in this situation?

A 15   **B** 8   **1A(b)(1)(A)**
C T **D** h

13 ____**C**____

14 Jan has a recipe that requires $2\frac{1}{2}$ cups of flour to make 72 chocolate chip cookies. She wants to make 90 cookies. How many cups of flour will she need? **3A(c)(2)(G)**

A $3\frac{1}{4}$ **B** $3\frac{1}{8}$

C 3   **D** $2\frac{3}{4}$

14 ____**B**____

15 Which of the following cannot be the side lengths of a triangle?

A 2 cm, 3 cm, 7 cm   **B** 4 cm, 5 cm, 6 cm   **10(8.16)(B)**
C 3 cm, 3 cm, 4 cm   **D** 5 cm, 5 cm, 5 cm

15 ____**A**____

16 A rectangle is three times as long as it is wide. How many lines of symmetry does the rectangle have? **7(8.7)(B)**

A 0   **B** 1
C 2   **D** 4

16 ____**C**____

TAKS Practice
Sample Test 1 (continued)

Read each question and choose the best answer. Then write the letter for the answer you have chosen in the blank at the right of each questin.

17 When a cube is increased in size, the area of each face is multiplied by 4. What happens to the volume of the cube? **8(8.10)(B)**

17 ___**D**___

A It is multiplied by 16.   **B** It is doubled.
C It is multiplied by 4.   **D** It is multiplied by 8.

18 What is the range of $f(x) = x + 8$? **2A(b)(2)(B)**

18 ___**B**___

A $x \geq 0$ **B** all real numbers
C all integers   **D** $y \leq 8$

19 The triangle shown at the right is to be dilated by a scale factor of 4. The center for the dilation is the origin. What are the coordinates of the vertices of the image? **6(8.6)(B)**

19 ___**D**___

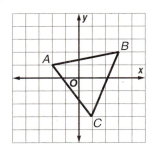

A $A'(2, 1), B'(7, 2), C'(5, -3)$
B $A'(-2, 5), B'(3, 6), C'(1, 1)$
C $A'(2, 5), B'(7, 6), C'(5, 1)$
D $A'(-8, 4), B'(12, 8), C'(4, -12)$

20 The Big West Cell telephone company offers 600 minutes per month for $29.95, 1000 minutes for $41.95, and 1500 minutes for $56.95. What is their charge per minute if their basic rate with no minutes is $11.95?

Record your answer and fill in the bubbles. Be sure to use the correct place value. **3A(c)(2)(F)**

20

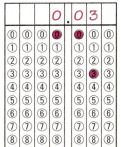

21 Dan and Vincent are having a free-throw shooting contest. This table shows the results.

21 ___**C**___

Player	Attempts	Number Made	Percent Made
Dan	10	6	60%
Vincent	5	4	80%

What is their combined average shooting percentage? **9(8.12)(A)**

A 80%   **B** 70%

C $66\frac{2}{3}\%$ **D** 60%

TAKS Practice
Sample Test 1 (continued)

Read each question and choose the best answer. Then write the letter for the answer you have chosen in the blank at the right of each question.

22 The floor of the gazebo shown in the diagram is a regular hexagon whose area is $24\sqrt{3}$ square feet. What is the volume of the gazebo? **8(8.8)(C)**

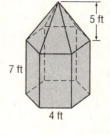

A $168\sqrt{3}$

B $208\sqrt{3}$

C $288\sqrt{3}$

D $416\sqrt{3}$

22 _____ **B**

23 About how many more injuries were there in 2001 than in 1997 according to this graph of all-terrain vehicle injuries?

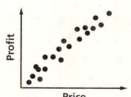

A 260   **9(8.12)(C)**

B 110

C 90

D twice as many

23 _____ **C**

24 Which of the following relationships is shown by this scatter plot? **2A(b)(2)(D)**

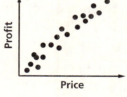

A As price increases, profit increases.

B As price increases, profit decreases.

C As price increases, profit remains constant.

D There is no relationship between price and profit.

24 _____ **A**

25 Which description fits the graph of $y = 14x + 6$? **2A(b)(2)(A)**

A line sloping up from left to the right

B line sloping down from left to the right

C horizontal line

D vertical line

25 _____ **A**

26 What is the perimeter of the trapezoid shown in the diagram? **7(8.7)(C)**

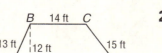

A 60 ft

B 70 ft

C 65 ft

D 61 ft

26 _____ **B**

TAKS Practice

Sample Test 1 (continued)

Read each question and choose the best answer. Then write the letter for the answer you have chosen in the blank at the right of each question.

27 Bob bought a car for $14,000. If the car depreciates $2000 per year, use an equation to find the value of the car after 4 years. **1A(b)(1)(3)**

Record your answer and fill in the bubbles. Be sure to use the correct place value.

27

| 6 | 0 | 0 | 0 | . | | |

28 Which sequence of numbers do you get if the expression $1 + (-1)^n$ describes the nth term of the sequence? **2A(b)(3)(B)**

A 0, 1, 0, 1, 0, 1, …
B 1, −1, 1, −1, 1, −1, …
C 0, 2, 0, 2, 0, 2, …
D −1, 2, −1, 2, −1, 2, …

28 ___C___

29 The equation $y = 8x + 20$ gives the cost y of printing x T-shirts. What does the slope represent? **3A(c)(2)(B)**

A cost per shirt
B retail price of a shirt
C set-up printing charge
D number of shirts

29 ___A___

30 Skippy wants to buy a DVD player. The regular price is $249.95, but it is on sale for 20 percent off. Which of the following is a reasonable estimate for the sale price without tax? **4A(c)(3)(C)**

A $500
B $300
C $230
D $200

30 ___D___

31 Simplify $a^{12} \div a^3$. **5A(d)(3)(A)**

A a^4
B a^6
C a^9
D a^{15}

31 ___C___

Go on

TAKS Practice

Sample Test 1 (continued)

Read each question and choose the best answer. Then write the letter for the answer you have chosen in the blank at the right of each question.

32 Which function describes the x and y values shown in the table?

1A(b)(1)(B)

x	1	2	3	4
y	-4	-1	2	5

A $y = 3x - 7$ **B** $y = 2x - 4$

C $y = -4x$ **D** $y = x - 5$

32 _____**A**_____

33 Greta needs a 25% solution of mosquito spray. If she has 10 gallons of solution that is 35% chemical, how many gallons of pure water must she add to reduce the mixture to 25% chemical? **9(8.3)(B)**

A 2 gal   **B** 4 gal

C 8 gal   **D** 10 gal

33 _____**B**_____

34 Roger is buying a new car costing $16,500. He can put $3000 down and pay $500 per month. Which of the following equations could you use to find how many months it will take Roger to pay for the car? **4A(c)(3)(A)**

A $3000 + 500x = 16{,}500$ **B** $3000x + 500 = 16{,}500$

C $\frac{16{,}500}{500} - 3000 = x$ **D** $16{,}500 + 3000x = 500$

34 _____**A**_____

35 How could the graph of $y = x^2 + 3$ be obtained from the graph of $y = x^2 - 4$? **5A(d)(1)(c)**

A Move the graph of $y = x^2 - 4$ to the left 7 units.

B Move the graph of $y = x^2 - 4$ to the right 7 units.

C Move the graph of $y = x^2 - 4$ up 7 units.

D Move the graph of $y = x^2 - 4$ down 7 units.

35 _____**C**_____

36 Study the fractions and decimals shown below. What is a reasonable conjecture for the number of digits in the repeating group of digits in the decimal for $\frac{1}{999{,}999}$? **10(8.16)(A)**

$\frac{4}{9} = 0.4444444444\ldots$

$\frac{17}{99} = 0.1717171717\ldots$

$\frac{4213}{999} = 4.217217217\ldots$

A 7   **B** 6

C 5   **D** 4

36 _____**B**_____

TAKS Practice

Sample Test 1 (continued)

Read each question and choose the best answer. Then write the letter for the answer you have chosen in the blank at the right of each question.

37 ABC Bank charges $0.40 per check and a service fee of $2.00 per month for their checking accounts. Using this graph of the relation between the number of checks written x and the cost of the checking account for one month y, about how much will the account cost George if he writes 6 checks during the month? **4A(c)(3)(B)**

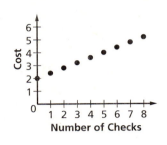

A $2.00   **B** $2.40
C $4.40   **D** $5.20

37 _____**C**_____

38 Ramon is wondering how many ways there are to use coins to make a dollar. Which is the best strategy for solving this problem? **9(8.13)(B)**

  A Find the number of ways to make 50¢ and multiply by 2.
  B Make an organized list of all the possibilities.
  C Write and solve an equation.
  D Draw a diagram.

38 _____**B**_____

39 In 2000–2001, the Texas Longhorns had the results shown in this table. If a game is chosen at random, what is the probability that it was a conference game or a win? **9(8.11)(A)**

	Conference	Non-Conference
Wins	10	12
Losses	6	6

A $\frac{14}{17}$ **B** $\frac{19}{17}$

C $\frac{5}{17}$ **D** $\frac{8}{17}$

39 _____**A**_____

40 What is the volume of a right triangular prism if the height is 4 and the bases have side lengths 5, 12, and 13? **8(8.8)(B)**
  A 312   **B** 240
  C 180   **D** 120

40 _____**D**_____

41 Which of the following is the height x of this cone?
  A $3\sqrt{34}$ **7(8.7)(C)**   **B** $2\sqrt{61}$
  C 12   **D** 6

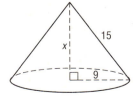

41 _____**C**_____

Go on

TAKS Practice

Sample Test 1 (continued)

*Read each question and choose the best answer. Then write the
letter for the answer you have chosen in the blank at the right of
each question.*

42 Use the data in this table. Look for a pattern. How many faces will a
regular octagonal prism have? **10(8.14)(C)**

Number of sides of base of prism	3	4	5	6	7
Number of faces	5	6	7	8	9

Record your answer and fill in the bubbles. Be sure to use the correct
place value.

42

Answer: 1 0 .

43 Which of these points lies on the *y*-axis? **6(8.7)(D)**

 A $(3, 0)$

 B $(0, -3)$

 C $(4, -1)$

 D $(-3, 2)$

43 ___**B**___

44 There are 380 people in an auditorium. Which is a correct conclusion
about how many people in the audience celebrate their birthdays on the
same day of the year? **10(8.16)(A)**

 A Exactly 2 people celebrate their birthdays on the same day.

 B At least 2 people celebrate their birthdays on the same day.

 C Exactly 15 people celebrate their birthdays on the same day.

 D No more than 2 people celebrate their birthdays on the same day.

44 ___**B**___

45 If the ratio of green lawn chairs to yellow lawn chairs is 7:9 and there
are a total of 352 lawn chairs, how many green lawn chairs are there?

 A 345   **3A(C)(2)(G)**

 B 198

 C 176

 D 154

45 ___**D**___

46 How is the graph of $y = x^2 + 2c$ related to the graph of $y = x^2 + c$ if
c is a negative number? **5A(d)(1)(C)**

 A It is 2 units higher in the coordinate plane.

 B It is 2 units lower in the coordinate plane.

 C It is $|c|$ units higher in the coordinate plane.

 D It is $|c|$ units lower in the coordinate plane.

46 ___**D**___

Go on

TAKS Practice
Sample Test 1 (continued)

Read each question and choose the best answer. Then write the letter for the answer you have chosen in the blank at the right of each question.

47 Which linear function has the graph with the greatest slope? **3A(c)(2)(C)**   47 ____**B**____

  A $y = -3x + 7$
  B $y = x - 9$
  C $y = -7x + 9$
  D $y = -5x + 10$

48 Rehan wants to draw a graph to show how the high temperatures varied during the school week last week. Which type of graph would be most appropriate? **10(8.15)(A)**   48 ____**D**____

Day	1	2	3	4	5
Temperature (°F)	62	85	87	72	69

  A circle graph with sectors for the number of days in the 60s, 70s, and 80s
  B bar graph with bars showing the number of days in the 60s, 70s, and 80s
  C box-and-whisker plot with temperatures on the horizontal axis
  D line graph with days on the horizontal axis and temperatures on the vertical axis

49 The number of bands in the Bayfest Parade was 6 more than twice the number of floats. If there were a total of 90 floats and bands in the parade, how many floats were there? **4A(c)(4)(A)**

Record your answer and fill in the bubbles. Be sure to use the correct place value.

49

50 If $(2, -7)$ is translated 5 units to the left and up 3, and then that image is reflected over the x-axis, what will be the coordinates of the final image point? **6(8.6)(B)**   50 ____**B**____

  A $(3, -4)$
  B $(-3, 4)$
  C $(7, 10)$
  D $(-7, -10)$

Go on

TAKS Practice
Sample Test 1 (continued)

**Read each question and choose the best answer. Then write the
letter for the answer you have chosen in the blank at the right of
each question.**

51 Which of the following is a top view of this object?

A

B

C

D

51 ___**C**___

7(8.7)(A)

52 Lou flew round trip from Houston to Dallas for $199. Two months later
the airline lowered all fares by 10 percent. How much is the new
round-trip fare? **9(8.1)(B)**

A $189

B $179.10

C $169

D $99.50

52 ___**B**___

53 A jar of coins contains only nickels and dimes. The total value of the
coins is $85.60. If d is the number of dimes and n is the number of
nickels, which equation describes the situation? **3A(c)(1)(C)**

A $10d + 5n = 8560$

B $0.10d + 0.05n = 8560$

C $10d + 5n = 85.60$

D $d + n = 85.60$

53 ___**A**___

54 Which of the following situations could be
represented by this graph? **1A(b)(1)(D)**

A the height h above the ground of a baseball
t seconds after it is thrown straight up in the air

B the height h above the ground of a baseball
t seconds after it is hit straight out to second base as a line drive

C the height h above the ground of a satellite that has been orbiting the
earth for t seconds

D the height h above the ground of a ball t seconds after it is dropped
from the top of the Tower of the Americas

54 ___**A**___

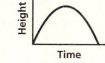

TAKS Practice
Sample Test 1 (continued)

Read each question and choose the best answer. Then write the letter for the answer you have chosen in the blank at the right of each question

55 Rusty has a model of a racecar. If the model car is 7 inches long and the scale is 1:18, how long would the real racecar be? **8(8.9)(B)**

A 25 in.   **B** 126 in.

C 18 ft   **D** 11 ft

55 ____**B**____

56 The Armadillos varsity cheerleading squad consists of 3 blonde juniors, 4 brunette juniors, 5 blonde seniors, and 3 brunette seniors. What is the probability that a cheerleader chosen at random is blonde or a senior?

A $\frac{1}{3}$ **B** $\frac{2}{5}$ **9(8.11)(B)**

C $\frac{5}{8}$ **D** $\frac{11}{15}$

56 ____**D**____

57 All spheres are similar. A jewelry maker has two imitation pearls that are spherical in shape and made of the same material. The larger pearl has a radius that is 4 times that of the smaller pearl. The smaller pearl has a mass of 0.3 grams. What is the mass in grams of the larger pearl?

A 0.15   **B** 1.2   **2A(b)(3)(A)**

C 4.8   **D** 19.2

57 ____**D**____

58 If these two trapezoids are similar, what is the value of *x*? **6(8.6)(A)**

A 21

B 15

C 14

D 12

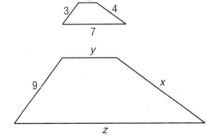

58 ____**D**____

59 Calculate $2^2 \cdot 5^3$, $2^3 \cdot 5^2$, $2^4 \cdot 5^2$, and $2^5 \cdot 5^2$. What is a reasonable conjecture for the number of zeros in the product for $2^9 \cdot 5^3$?

A 3   **B** 6   **10(8.16)(A)**

C 9   **D** 12

59 ____**A**____

60 What is the surface area of this box? **8(8.8)(A)**

A 118 in²   **B** 236 in²

C 240 in²   **D** 480 in²

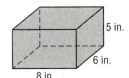

60 ____**B**____

TAKS Practice
Sample Test 2

Read each question and choose the best answer. Then write the letter for the answer you have chosen in the blank at the right of each question.

1 If $f(x) = -x^2 + 8x - 2$, what is $f(2)$? **2A(b)(4)(A)**
  A 22
  B 18
  C 14
  D 10

1   **D**

2 Charlie went to Juarez, Mexico, on a shopping trip. He bought silver rings at $5 each and baskets at $8 each. If he bought a total of 19 items and spent $131, how many baskets did he buy? **4A(c)(4)(A)**
  A 7
  B 12
  C 13
  D 15

2   **B**

3 Robin built a dartboard like the one shown in the diagram. If he throws a dart that hits the board, what is the probability that it lands in the shaded area? **8(8.8)(C)**
  A $\frac{1}{3}$
  B $\frac{7}{12}$
  C $\frac{49}{144}$
  D $\frac{5}{18}$

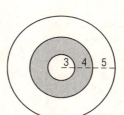

3   **D**

4 Maggie is building a dollhouse for her granddaughter. The scale is $\frac{1}{2}$ inch = 1 foot. If the living room of the actual house is 20 feet long, how long should the living room of the dollhouse be? **8(8.9)(B)**
  A 10 in.
  B 40 in.
  C 10 ft
  D 40 ft

4   **A**

5 Lucy's boat is floating down the river at the water park at 2 miles per hour. What is the independent variable in this situation? **1A(b)(1)(A)**
  A the time when she got into the boat
  B the speed of the boat
  C the distance she has traveled
  D the time that she has been in the boat

5   **D**

TAKS Practice
Sample Test 2 (continued)

Read each question and choose the best answer. Then write the letter for the answer you have chosen in the blank at the right of each question.

6 A baseball diamond is a square with sides that are 90 feet long. How many feet is the diagonal of the square? Round your answer to two decimal places. **8(8.9)(A)**

Record your answer and fill in the bubbles. Be sure to use the correct place value.

6

	1	2	7	.	2	8	
⓪	⓪	⓪	⓪		⓪	⓪	⓪
①	●	①	①		①	①	①
②	②	●	②		●	②	②
③	③	③	③		③	③	③
④	④	④	④		④	④	④
⑤	⑤	⑤	⑤		⑤	⑤	⑤
⑥	⑥	⑥	⑥		⑥	⑥	⑥
⑦	⑦	⑦	●		⑦	⑦	⑦
⑧	⑧	⑧	⑧		⑧	●	⑧
⑨	⑨	⑨	⑨		⑨	⑨	⑨

7 What are the coordinates of the image of $A(3, 5)$ when the point is reflected across the line $y = -x$? **6(8.6)(B)**

7 _____ **B**

A $(5, 3)$ **B** $(-5, -3)$
C $(3, -5)$ **D** $(-3, -5)$

8 Duke and Enrique work at the same lumberyard. Each works at most 40 hours per week, and the amount that each of them earns varies directly with the number of hours worked. The graph of the function for Duke's earnings has a slope of 8. The graph for Enrique has a slope of 12. How do their earnings compare when they work the same number of hours?

8 _____ **A**

A Enrique earns 1.5 times as much as Duke.   **3A(c)(2)(F)**
B Enrique earns 0.5 times as much as Duke.
C Enrique earns $160 more than Duke.
D Enrique earns $40 more than Duke.

9 What is the sixth term in the sequence $-4, -1, 2, 5, \ldots$? **2A(b)(3)(B)**

9 _____ **C**

A 5   **B** 8
C 11   **D** 14

10 The areas of two similar rectangles are in a ratio of 4:9. The length of the smaller rectangle is 6. What is the length of the larger rectangle?

10 _____ **B**

A $13\frac{1}{2}$ **B** 9   **8(8.10(A)**
C 4   **D** $2\frac{2}{3}$

11 What is an equation of the line that passes through the points at $(2, 5)$ and $(-1, 6)$? **3A(c)(2)(D)**

11 _____ **A**

A $y - 5 = -\frac{1}{3}(x - 2)$ **B** $y + 5 = -\frac{1}{3}(x + 2)$
C $y - 5 = 3(x - 2)$ **D** $y - 6 = -3(x + 1)$

TAKS Practice
Sample Test 2 (continued)

Read each question and choose the best answer. Then write the letter for the answer you have chosen in the blank at the right of each question.

12 Which situation could be represented by this graph? **2A(b)(2)(C)**

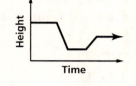

A A racecar on the speedway crashes into the wall and stops.

B Bero walks in the field, stops to eat a sandwich, then continues walking.

C A man runs up the steps, stops at the top, then runs back down faster than he ran up.

D A man walks on a level sidewalk, then descends the stairs to the Riverwalk, walks along the river, then goes back up the next stairs and continues walking.

12 _____**D**_____

13 Victoria has a rule for classifying whole numbers as "star numbers" or "not star numbers." What is a possible rule she might be using to decide whether a number is a star number? **9(8.12)(A)**

Star Numbers	Not Star Numbers
30	1
5907	125
6000	8
400,231	27
520,908	529,298

A The number is not a perfect cube.

B The number is less than 500,000.

C The number has at least one digit that is 0.

D The number is divisible by 3.

13 _____**C**_____

14 Carmen was in the forest with her camera to photograph animals. She took pictures of 3 ducks, 2 geese, and 8 white-tailed deer. If she chooses two of the pictures at random for a poster, what is the probability that both will be of deer? **9(8.11)(A)**

A $\frac{8}{13}$

B $\frac{56}{169}$

C $\frac{1}{4}$

D $\frac{14}{39}$

14 _____**D**_____

15 Nelsons manufactures baseballs at a cost of $7.50 each with fixed costs of $10,000. If one baseball sells for $12, how many must they sell to make a profit of $12,000? **4A(c)(3)(B)**

A 1000

B 1834

C 2667

D 4889

15 _____**D**_____

TAKS Practice

Sample Test 2 (continued) ─────────────────

Read each question and choose the best answer. Then write the letter for the answer you have chosen in the blank at the right of each question.

16 If you fold the pattern shown at the right to make a closed three-dimensional figure, what kind of figure will you get? **7(8.7)(A)**

  A hexagonal pyramid
  B triangular pyramid
  C hexagonal prism
  D triangular prism

16 ___**A**___

17 Which point is included in the graph of $2x + y \leq 7$? **4A(c)(3)(C)**

  A $(-4, 16)$
  B $(2, 4)$
  C $(5, -2)$
  D $(-2, 13)$

17 ___**C**___

18 Which of the following shapes is similar to this triangle?

  A   **B**

  C   **D**   **6(8.6)(A)**

18 ___**C**___

19 Larry wants to draw a triangle that has sides 6 inches and 11 inches long. Which could be the length of the third side? **10(8.16)(B)**

  A 18 in.
  B 8 in.
  C 5 in.
  D 3 in.

19 ___**B**___

20 Which of the following would be an appropriate unit for describing the area of the floor of your math classroom? **10(8.15)(A)**

  A square feet
  B cubic feet
  C square millimeters
  D acres

20 ___**A**___

TAKS Practice
Sample Test 2 (continued)

Read each question and choose the best answer. Then write the letter for the answer you have chosen in the blank at the right of each question.

21 If the ratio of the sides of 2 cubes is 5:9, what is the ratio of their volumes?   21 ____**C**____

    A 5:9   **B** 25:81   **8(8.10)(B)**

    C 125:729   **D** 625:6561

22 What is the volume of a cylinder with a height 10 inches and a base with   22 ____**D**____
a radius of 4 inches? **8(8.8)(B)**

    A 16π in^3 **B** 40π in^3

    C 80π in^3 **D** 160π in^3

23 What is the solution of $-\frac{2}{3}x + 5 < 7$? **4A(c)(3)(B)**   23 ____**B**____

    A $x < -3$ **B** $x > -3$

    C $x < -\frac{4}{3}$ **D** $x > -\frac{4}{3}$

24 Which of these is a quadratic function? **2A(b)(2)(A)**   24 ____**A**____

    A $y = 4x^2$ **B** $y = 4x^4$

    C $y = 4x$ **D** $y = 4$

25 Bill is driving a truck across the Texas panhandle on U.S. 40, a distance   25 ____**D**____
of 176 miles. If he drives at 65 miles per hour, how many hours will it
take him to cross the panhandle? Round your answer to the nearest tenth.

    A 707.7   **B** 190.7   **4A(c)(3)(A)**

    C 3.2   **D** 2.7

26 The table gives data about the scores on an algebra test in Mr. Harley's   26 ____**D**____
class. What is the probability that a student chosen at random was a boy
who got an A on the test? **9(8.11)(B)**

Grade	Score	Number of Boys	Number of Girls
A	90–100	3	4
B	80–89	6	8
C	70–79	10	7
D	60–69	1	3
F	0–59	2	1

    A $\frac{26}{45}$ **B** $\frac{3}{22}$

    C $\frac{4}{45}$ **D** $\frac{1}{15}$

Go on

TAKS Practice

Sample Test 2 (continued)

Read each question and choose the best answer. Then write the letter for the answer you have chosen in the blank at the right of each question.

27 Mario's coin collection contains nickels, dimes, and quarters. He has five times as many quarters as nickels and fifteen fewer dimes than quarters. The total value of his collection is $29.10. What is the least number of variables you would need to use to write and solve one or more equations to find the number of coins of each kind? **2A(b)(3)(A)**

A 3   **B** 2
C 1   **D** 0

27 ___**C**___

28 What percent of the students scored between 90 and 98 on this quiz? Use the data in the box-and-whisker plot. **2A(b)(2)(D)**

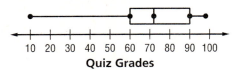

Quiz Grades

Record your answer and fill in the bubbles. Be sure to use the correct place value.

28

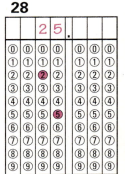

29 If $(-50, a)$ is in Quadrant II, what kind of number must a be? **6(8.7)(D)**

A negative   **B** positive
C zero   **D** rational

29 ___**B**___

30 A soft drink costs $3 and a hot dog costs $4 at the baseball park. The equation $3x + 4y = 30$ describes the relationship between the number of soft drinks x and the number of hot dogs y that can be purchased for $30. What does the x-intercept of the graph of the equation represent?

A cost of the hot dogs   **3A(c)(2)(B)**
B cost of the soft drinks
C number of soft drinks if no hot dogs are purchased
D number of hot dogs if no soft drinks are purchased

30 ___**C**___

31 Jack earns a salary of x dollars per hour at the discount store. He gets time and a half for overtime hours if he works more than 35 hours during the week. Which equation gives his earnings s for a week when he works h hours of overtime? **1A(b)(1)(E)**

A $s = 35x + xh$ **B** $s = 35x + 1.5h$
C $s = 35x + 1.5h - 52.5$ **D** $s = 35x + 1.5xh$

31 ___**D**___

Go on

TAKS Practice

Sample Test 2 (continued)

Read each question and choose the best answer. Then write the letter for the answer you have chosen in the blank at the right of each question.

32 The Sleepy Bear Farm plants c acres of cotton and w acres of wheat. They plant four times as many acres of cotton as wheat. The total number of acres planted is 2000. Which system of equations could be used to find the number of acres of wheat? **4A(c)(4)(A)**

  A $c + 4w = 2000$
     $c + w = 8000$

  B $c + w = 2000$
     $w = 4c$

  C $4c + w = 2000$
     $c + w = 8000$

  D $c + w = 2000$
     $c = 4w$

32 _____ **D** _____

33 The enrollment in 1999 at Texas A & M University was 43,389 and the enrollment at Rice University was 4318. The enrollment at Texas A & M was about what percent of the enrollment at Rice? **9(8.3)(B)**

  A 1000%
  B 900%
  C 100%
  D 10%

33 _____ **A** _____

34 Which equation is true for all values of x? **10(8.16)(B)**

  A $(x - 3)^2 = x^2 + 9$
  B $(x - 3)^2 = x^2 - 9$
  C $(x - 3)^2 = x^2 + 6x + 9$
  D $(x - 3)^2 = x^2 - 6x + 9$

34 _____ **D** _____

35 How many lines of symmetry are there for a regular polygon with seven sides? **7(8.7)(B)**

Record your answer and fill in the bubbles. Be sure to use the correct place value.

35

			7	.			
⓪	⓪	⓪	⓪		⓪	⓪	⓪
①	①	①	①		①	①	①
②	②	②	②		②	②	②
③	③	③	③		③	③	③
④	④	④	④		④	④	④
⑤	⑤	⑤	⑤		⑤	⑤	⑤
⑥	⑥	⑥	⑥		⑥	⑥	⑥
⑦	⑦	⑦	⑦		⑦	⑦	⑦
⑧	⑧	⑧	⑧		⑧	⑧	⑧
⑨	⑨	⑨	⑨		⑨	⑨	⑨

36 Dolores and Ozzie are going to the carnival. They can either pay an admission price of $11.95 each, which includes all rides, or pay $3 each at the door and 75 cents per ride. Which inequality could be used to find how many rides they must each go on in order to save money by paying the all-inclusive admission price? **4A(c)(3)(A)**

  A $0.75x < 11.95$
  B $0.75x > 11.95$
  C $0.75x + 3.00 > 11.95$
  D $0.75x + 3.00 < 11.95$

36 _____ **C** _____

Go on

TAKS Practice
Sample Test 2 (continued)

Read each question and choose the best answer. Then write the letter for the answer you have chosen in the blank at the right of each question.

37 The table shows average high temperatures, in degrees Fahrenheit, in December and June for six U.S. cities. To see whether there is a correlation between the December and June data, which would be the best method to use? **10(8.14)(C)**   37 ____**B**____

December	23	36	56	75	40	6
June	70	78	92	80	85	70

A Draw a box-and-whisker plot.
B Draw a scatter plot.
C Draw a circle graph.
D Draw a bar graph.

38 Which function contains the points at $(3, 8)$, $(-2, 3)$, and $(0, -1)$ in its graph? **1A(b)(1)(B)**   38 ____**C**____

A $f(x) = 2x^2 - 1$
B $f(x) = 2x^2 + x - 1$
C $f(x) = x^2 - 1$
D $f(x) = x - 1$

39 If lettuce costs x cents per head and carrots cost 99¢ per bunch, which of these equations gives the total cost c of 3 bunches of carrots and 6 heads of lettuce? **3A(c)(1)(C)**   39 ____**A**____

A $c = 99(3) + 6x$
B $c = 99 + 6x$
C $c = 99(3) + x$
D $c = 99 + x$

40 If the Spurs win 80 percent of their 82 games and the Cowboys win 90 percent of their 16 games, which team will win more games?   40 ____**A**____

A Spurs   **9(8.13)(B)**
B Cowboys
C They will win the same number of games.
D Not possible to determine

41 What is the image of the point $(3, 5)$ reflected over the line $x = -1$ and then translated up 4 units and to the right 2 units? **6(8.6)(B)**   41 ____**B**____

A $(-1, 7)$ **B** $(-3, 9)$
C $(5, 1)$ **D** $(7, -5)$

Go on

TAKS Practice

Sample Test 2 (continued)

Read each question and choose the best answer. Then write the letter for the answer you have chosen in the blank at the right of each question.

42 Lee works for a department store in Dallas. He earns 8% commission on his sales. Which of the following functions represents his commission c on sales of s dollars? **1A(b)(1)(C)**

A $c = 8s$ **B** $c = 8 + s$

C $c = 0.08 + s$ **D** $c = 0.08s$

42 ___**D**___

43 What is the product of 8.4×10^7 and 5×10^4 written in scientific notation? **5A(d)(3)(A)**

A 42×10^{28} **B** 4.2×10^{12}

C 4.2×10^{11} **D** 4.2×10^3

43 ___**B**___

44 The cost of peaches varies directly with the number of peaches bought. If 6 peaches cost $1.74, how much would 15 peaches cost? **3A(c)(2)(G)**

Record your answer and fill in the bubbles. Be sure to use the correct place value.

44

45 Find the volume of this 45° wedge cut from the cylindrical block of cheese shown in the diagram.

A 452.39 in^3

B 75.40 in^3 **8(8.8)(C)**

C 56.55 in^3

D 37.70 in^3

45 ___**C**___

46 Five friends all live on the same street. Art lives between Bladimir and Curt. David lives farther from Art than from Curt, but closer to Art than to Burt. Burt lives between Eduardo and Art. Their basketball coach wants to know how many of the boys live between David and Eduardo. What is the most reasonable strategy for solving this problem? **3A(c)(2)(B)**

A Draw a diagram.   **B** Make a table.

C Make an organized list.   **D** Work backward.

46 ___**A**___

TAKS Practice
Sample Test 2 (continued)

Read each question and choose the best answer. Then write the letter for the answer you have chosen in the blank at the right of each question.

47 Mai Ling was calculating the probability of getting a sum of 3 when two fair dice are tossed. Which would be a reasonable method she could use to solve this problem? **10(8.14)(B)**

  A Toss a pair of dice 10 times and record how many times the sum is 3.
  B Calculate the probability that one die is a 3 and double this answer.
  C Count all the ways 3 can be written as the sum of two whole numbers, and then divide by 36.
  D Make a chart of the possible sums for two dice. Count how many times the sum is 3, then divide by 36.

47   **D**

48 Which of the following situations could be represented by this graph? **1A(b)(1)(D)**

  A cost of a beef roast as a function of weight
  B temperature of a jug of water as a function of time in the refrigerator
  C distance run in a marathon as a function of the time run
  D time to cook a chicken as a function of weight

48   **B**

49 A copy machine can make a copy of a document every 3 seconds. How many copies can it make in 17 minutes? **10(8.14)(A)**

  A 1024   **B** 340
  C 240   **D** 51

49   **B**

50 Mikayla earns money by walking dogs for people who do not have time to do it themselves. She earns $95 per day. Her income for a year is a function of the number of days d that she walks dogs. What is a reasonable domain for this function? **2A(b)(2)(B)**

  A all real numbers d such that $d \le 365$
  B all real numbers d such that $-365 \le d \le 365$
  C all whole numbers d such that $0 \le d \le 365$
  D all whole numbers d such that $0 \le d \le 95(365)$

50   **C**

51 Joe is thinking of a kind of number. $\sqrt{4}$, $\sqrt{9}$, and $\sqrt{49}$ are this kind of number, but $\sqrt{5}$, $\sqrt{11}$, and $\sqrt{60}$ are not. Which of the following is probably another example of the kind of number he is thinking of?

  A $\sqrt{200}$ **B** $\sqrt{81}$ **10(8.16)(A)**
  C $\sqrt{40}$ **D** $\sqrt{17}$

51   **B**

Go on

TAKS Practice
Sample Test 2 (continued)

Read each question and choose the best answer. Then write the letter for the answer you have chosen in the blank at the right of each question.

52 Maya sells her special chili for $4.25 a quart. How much will her sales be if she sells 16 gallons? **3A(c)(2)(G)**

  A $272
  B $136
  C $68
  D $34

52   **A**

53 What is the value of x in this right triangle? **7(8.7)(C)**

  A $2\sqrt{2}$
  B 4
  C $\sqrt{34}$
  D 6

53   **C**

54 Approximately 1.5×10^6 million Mexican free-tail bats live under the Congress bridge in Austin in the summer. If the bats consume about 2×10^4 pounds of insects each night, about how many pounds of insects does each bat eat? Round to the nearest thousandth. **5A(d)(3)(A)**

Record your answer and fill in the bubbles. Be sure to use the correct place value.

54

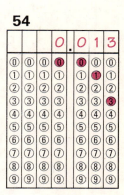

55 What is the x-intercept of the linear function determined by the data in this table? **3A(C)(2)(F)**

x	4	−2	10
y	−6	−1	−11

  A 0
  B $-2\frac{2}{3}$
  C $-3\frac{1}{5}$
  D −4

55   **C**

56 What is the perimeter of a rectangular yard that is 136.4 meters long and 71.8 meters wide? **9(8.1)(B)**

  A 9793.52 m
  B 4896.76 m
  C 545.6 m
  D 416.4 m

56   **D**

Name _____   Date _____

TAKS Practice
Sample Test 2 (continued)

Read each question and choose the best answer. Then write the letter for the answer you have chosen in the blank at the right of each question.

57 A group of 12 Girl Scouts bought tickets to see a musical. Main floor tickets are $60 each, and first balcony tickets are $35 each. If the total price of the tickets was $520, how many main floor tickets did they buy?

A 0
B 4
C 8
D 1

4A(c)(3)(C)

57 ____**B**____

58 Which of the following is the graph of $y = -2x^2 + 1$? **5A(d)(1)(C)**

58 ____**A**____

A
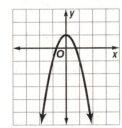

B
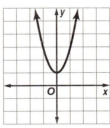

C
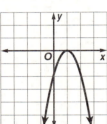

D
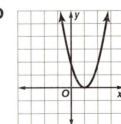

59 Which function has a graph that does not touch or cross the x-axis?

A $y = x^2$
B $y = x^2 - 4$
C $y = x^2 - 1$
D $y = x^2 + 2$

5A(d)(1)(C)

59 ____**D**____

60 To tessellate a plane means to cover it with congruent non-overlapping shapes. Which of the following figures would tessellate a plane?

60 ____**A**____

A

B

7(8.7)(B)

C

D

STOP